THE INVISIBLE TOUCH

The Four Keys to Modern Marketing

HARRY BECKWITH

BUSINESS PLUS

NEW YORK   BOSTON

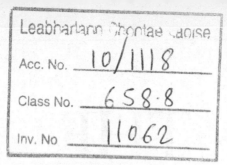
Copyright © 2000 by Harry Beckwith
All rights reserved. Except as permitted under the U.S. Copyright Act
of 1976, no part of this publication may be reproduced, distributed, or
transmitted in any form or by any means, or stored in a database or
retrieval system, without the prior written permission of the publisher.

Business Plus
Hachette Book Group
237 Park Avenue
New York, NY 10017

Visit our website at www.HachetteBookGroup.com.

Printed in the United States of America

Originally published in hardcover by Hachette Book Group.

First Trade Edition: August 2009
10 9 8 7 6 5 4 3 2 1

Business Plus is an imprint of Grand Central Publishing.
The Business Plus name and logo are trademarks of Hachette Book
Group, Inc.

The Library of Congress has cataloged the hardcover edition as follows:

Beckwith, Harry.
   The invisible touch : the four keys to modern marketing / Harry
Beckwith.
      p. cm.
   ISBN 978-0-446-52417-9
      1. Service industries—Marketing.   I. Title.

HD9980.5 B423 2000
658.8—dc21   99-048663

ISBN 978-0-446-69983-9 (pbk.)

Book design by Giorgetta Bell McRee

To you, Mom.

I heard you.

CONTENTS

CONTENTS

Contents

CONTENTS

Introduction

The lures of partial-celebrity are tempting. For both your sake and mine, however, I hope to resist them.

I wrote *Selling the Invisible* from obscurity. A few hundred clients, friends, and acquaintances knew me. On the morning the book first appeared on the shelves, March 5, 1997, our clients reached from Greensboro to San Francisco, but 80 percent worked within view of the IDS building in midtown Minneapolis.

As I look back on how much has changed since then, I realize my first book offers this lesson to service providers: Write one. If a book sells nicely, an author's life changes.

Letters arrived postmarked from towns we'd never heard of (Valley, Nebraska? Kosciusko, Mississippi?). Callers spoke in dialects we'd never heard of (Singapore has a dialect? Pakistan?). Both often overflowed with compliments. Those incredible compliments actually poured in, unsolicited. None was written by an old friend, by someone whose back I'd scratched first, or by Jimmy Franco, Warner Books' fine publicist.

This welcome response brought with it a temptation.

The temptation is to think I know everything

now, and to write a book from that narrower perspective. Like fatigue narrows a distance runner's peripheral vision, the label "expert" can limit an author's. The author starts looking inside, confident of finding wisdom there, drawing on what he already "knows." Thus diverted, he misses the critical insights outside his tunnel vision.

This book does look closer to home. Its emphasis on my experience—as a service provider, a client, and an adviser to services—reflects how the months spent on the first book changed my perspective.

Selling the Invisible drew heavily on larger businesses such as McDonald's. As the book evolved, however, my perspective evolved, too. It was ready to change completely; the slightest nudge would do that.

Then the nudge came.

In the summer of 1997, I called Alan Webber, the editor of the magazine *Fast Company*. In the course of a nice phone conversation, we agreed to a swap: two signed copies of *Selling the Invisible* in exchange for a *Fast Company* denim hat.

The following Monday, my receptionist carried a small box into my office. The conspicuous return address said *Fast Company*. I tore open the box, knowing what was inside.

I reached in, pulled out the hat, and noticed an enigmatic slogan on the back of it: *Work Is Per-*

sonal. I viewed those three words, perplexed. What did they mean? What could they mean?

The force of those words soon imploded in my head: Work *is* personal.

Work is not about business; it's about us. The human dimension of business—the messy, emotional, utterly human dimension—is not merely important; *it is all-encompassing.* As a result, we must plunge into the world of feelings—truly frightening territory.

In our search for critical insights into business, particularly marketing, we can learn from Peter Drucker, Philip Kotler, and Theodore Levitt. But we can learn just as much from Shakespeare, and perhaps even more from Daniel Goleman's bus driver (see page 40). Business provides one stage on which we act out the human drama. We understand the stage; we know far less about the drama. Fortunately, we can find the "texts" that can teach about that script in front of us every day: a cabby rushing us through downtown Chicago; your four-year-old son reacting to some colors but not others; Hamlet battling his demons.

The first good lesson of marketing, then, may be this. *Look.* Just look around. And look *carefully.* See what is there—rather than what you expected to find.

It is not a perfect method. Nothing is. Among other things, you can conclude far too much from the little you see. You see an exception, for example, but declare it the rule. You see something, write a book, and then notice yourself being quoted. You feel terrified. You realize that much of what you have regarded as wisdom all these years was just other people quoting other people like you—people making their best educated guesses.

The shock is enough to make you stop reading.

I am not expressing false modesty, or modesty at all. I wrote this book with conviction. The evidence makes every conclusion seem almost irrefutable. But like most people, I often assemble the evidence after my conclusions, not before them. I usually stick by my guns, even after my bullets are gone. Like all people, I am puzzling even to myself but deeply engaged in trying to solve this puzzle. It helps me to recognize patterns that help build businesses. Like everyone, I yield to emotions and idiosyncrasies; reason badly; succumb to impulse, influence, and other false prophets; and regularly act against my own self-interest.

With those disclaimers, I begin this book.

I do not intend this as some final word, but as some first ones. Many who have followed this advice have enjoyed either sudden luck or well-earned success. Most of this advice reflects the experience of the twentieth century's smartest and most successful service marketers: Ray Kroc and Walt Disney. These pages offer fuel for growth and food for thought, and this final reminder: Those two are not mutually exclusive.

The wise marketer looks for buffets filled with food for thought: the isolated events, curious behaviors, odd trends, and tiny bits of data, all of whose relevance is unclear. The marketer who can assemble a shrewd blend of this information can create a power salad: an idea, strategy, or tactic that changes a business. Sometimes, the answer we need is not the answer, but another perspective on the problem. You see a slogan on a hat, for example—"Work is personal." Suddenly, the fog lifts.

On behalf of the many people who have contributed so generously to this book and to my life, I hope you find pieces here that make a sudden difference, and perspectives that help you eventually, and forever.

*   *   *

It's a warm fall evening in 1970. I hand eight dollar bills to a woman in a glass ticket booth, and almost sprint with my girlfriend Annie to our seats in the sixth row of Stanford's Memorial Auditorium. Laura Nyro plays tonight. We have been in thrall to the singer-songwriter since we first heard her album *Eli and the Thirteenth Confession,* with songs like *"Eli's Comin',"* *"Stoned Soul Picnic,"* and *"Woman's Blues."* We sit. We fidget. We cross our legs, then uncross them, then repeat the drill. We cannot wait to be enthralled in person.

It doesn't happen.

Almost nothing happens, in fact. The curtain rises. Nyro sits with her right profile to us. She remains in that profile, rarely budging except for her arms, for ninety minutes. Looking across the stage and never toward the audience, Nyro plays the piano and sings. After each song she hurriedly introduces her next song; she looks at no one. She sings all her songs we love. But while the songs sound the same as they do on the LP, we hear them much differently.

Our simple reaction speaks volumes about the differences between services and products, and the differences in marketing them.

Laura Nyro's album is a *product*. We spent $4.98 for *Eli*—for the way her lyrics, melodies, and production values appealed to our senses and souls. We bought this product for its technical features: its words, its tunes, her voice.

When Nyro gave her concert, we were buying something different. She was supposed to be providing a *service*. We were paying for an experience and a relationship. Unfortunately, she never connected with us. We felt incomplete and left dissatisfied. Her technical quality had not changed, but our experience had—for the worse.

Laura Nyro knew how to create a marketable product. But in her concerts, her service, she committed the blunder that many artists, architects, and millions of other service people commit every day. She assumed that only the quality of her product mattered. Everything else—presentation, connection, human contact—she regarded as superfluous. Maybe she considered all that to be too commercial.

And so she failed.

This bygone concert by this now deceased artist illuminates an immediate issue: the difference between services and products, a difference *Selling the Invisible* touched on:

Products are made; services are *delivered*.

Products are used; services are *experienced*.

Products possess physical characteristics we can evaluate before we buy; services *do not even exist before we buy* them. We request them, often paying in advance. Then we receive them.

And finally, products are impersonal: bricks, mortar, pens, car seats, fruit—things with no human connection to us. Services, by contrast, are *personal*—often frighteningly so. A service relationship touches our essence and reveals the people involved: provider and customer. For that reason, a service marketing course belongs in the School of the Humanities. Service marketers, like humanities scholars, strive to answer this question:

"What does it mean to be a human being?"

No one knows exactly. We know less than we assume we do, and far less than marketing research suggests we do.

But in business, he who hesitates is lost. We cannot wait for the Absolute Truths, of which there are so few. We must settle for some Apparently Useful Premises: assumptions that usually produce good results. This book attempts to uncover those AUPs, and eventually deliver to you, the reader, their many benefits—of which financial reward is only one.

You may object to the Laura Nyro analogy. "My service is not like a concert," you say. But it is. Your customers buy more than the simple delivery of some basic service; they buy the entire experience. If people sought only basic services, Caribou's double cappuccinos would cost less than Taco Bell's burritos, because the raw ingredients and labor cost less. Consumers buy more than things; they purchase connections. (The remarkably named businesswoman Silver Rose described this perfectly. "I think adults invented work," she observed, "so that they could play together all day.")

Our lives seem increasingly disconnected. Our grown children move farther from home; technology reduces direct contact with people. Our drive for connection grows more intense. Making genuine, human connections becomes more important everywhere—not least of all in our businesses every day.

Most workers no longer build; they serve. We have become a service economy, right down to the business unit, and the smallest business unit of all: the individual. We provide a service that we offer to the market—to clients, prospects, customers, contractors, and employers.

We give concerts. The question is, how much better can we give them?

RESEARCH AND
ITS LIMITS

The Frame of Mind: Humble Openness

What can we know?

This question is so fundamental that an entire branch of philosophy, epistemology, has evolved around it. What is knowledge? And how can you know that your plan will work?

You can't. In this time when even great physicists—indeed, especially great physicists—are wracked with doubt, total certainty signals foolishness—in fact, certainty can be fatal.

Too easily, we decide that other people are like us. We project our own desires and attitudes onto entire markets. We trust our observations.

But often what we believe we see is not really there.

You can find powerful evidence of this phenomenon in courts of law. Every day, eyewitnesses to crime testify, offering their observations with assurance, and we trust them. When we read "An eyewitness identified John Doe as the assailant," then learn John Doe was found innocent, we are alarmed. We scream, "Reform the justice system." We think nothing could be more reliable than an eyewitness. What we should reform, however, is our view of eyewitnesses and our faith in human perception.

To shake your own faith in your own perception, read Jon Krakauer's best-seller *Into Thin Air.* (Given how many copies of the book have been sold, perhaps I should say "reread.") At one point, Krakauer interviewed three participants about a key moment in that fatal attempt to ascend Mount Everest. From those three people, you would expect that the real facts would emerge.

Something else emerged instead: a reminder of our frailty. The three could not agree on the time of the event. Nor could they agree on precisely, or even approximately, what was said. And none agreed on who else was present at the time!

In the immortal words of Firesign Theater, "What is reality?" Lily Tomlin may have answered that best in her solo stage show *The Search for Signs of Intelligent Life in the Universe,* written by Jane Wagner.

"After all," Tomlin's bag lady character muses, "what is reality anyway? Nothin' but a collective hunch."

Tomlin may have exaggerated, but the successful marketer should question virtually everything—especially her own observations. The brilliant marketer acts with humble openness. She willingly believes she may be wrong, accepts other ways of thinking, and recognizes that prospects may think much differently than she does.

Still, we cling to the faith that the answers are out there, waiting for research ingenious enough to find them.

Certainty is fatal.

The Unreliable Subject

But research may be one of our weakest tools. Take two examples, one older, one recent.

One fall day in 1962, my mother received a call from Phoenix, Arizona. The world was smaller then, and a call to us in Neah-Kah-Nie, Oregon (population 123), from anyplace more distant than Portland was an event. The caller was from the A.C. Nielsen Company, the people who measure TV audiences and issue the ratings. They wanted us to be a Nielsen family.

My mother happily obliged the exotic caller. Several days later, we received a detailed pamphlet that looked like a day planner, with instructions on how to fill out the TV diary. We were asked to watch whichever shows we normally watched and record how many people were watching the show during each fifteen-minute interval.

Being a competitive and goal-oriented bunch,

we Beckwiths were eager to be among the best Nielsen families ever. We painstakingly filled out each line of the diary, quarter-hour segment by quarter-hour segment, with the names of the shows that we watched. There was only one problem.

These weren't the shows we normally watched. Yes, we did watch our usual shows, like *The Defenders*. But if there was a time slot during which we normally watched nothing, then—anxious to be conscientious television watchers, especially of the "better" programs—we would watch whatever looked best. And so during those two weeks in the fall of 1962, the Beckwiths of Neah-Kah-Nie, Oregon, watched at least ten TV shows we'd never watched before, and never watched again. Programs, we suspect, that looked awfully good in the ratings that year.

What were we doing? We were letting the fact we were being observed influence what we did. We were not being who we were, but who we wanted to appear to be under the circumstances—which in our case was a family who watched quality television.

People who know they are being studied change what they do.

In 1999, Starbucks wanted to know what its customers thought. So the company commissioned researchers to question them in person, on the spot. Many readers have already detected the flaw in this research design. If on behalf of a host you ask party guests their opinions of the party, they will gush.

Granted, the people behind the counter at Starbucks are not party hosts. But they *are* hosts, and they *are* standing near the guests, whom they have just earnestly served a warm latte, trying their best. As a guest, will you tell the researchers that your latte is merely good, the earnest girl's service only adequate, and the store ambience acceptable but in need of work?

As the person behind the counter, you know you are being observed. How does that affect you? Do you act normally? Are you providing a truly representative experience?

These two examples illustrate a basic rule of research: Research changes its own results. Natural scientists originally observed this phenomenon, and the first discoverer gave it his name: the Heisenberg uncertainty principle. But in the realm of the natural sciences, at least some basic rules like gravity, relativity, and the laws of thermodynamics are at work; if a researcher can affect the relationships among protons and neutrons, what does this tell us about the validity of research into people's attitudes and behaviors?

It tells us that research alters those apparent attitudes and behaviors.

This phenomenon explains another regularly observed occurrence. Researchers tend to find what they are looking for. Again, natural scientists have noticed this in their own research; they call this phenomenon "the participative universe." Physicist John Wheeler Archibald observed that when you look for particular information, you tend to find it. You lose your ability to see other information, or to reach other conclusions—especially contradictory information or conclusions.

We learn what we hoped to.

This has profound meaning when we think about marketing "research." It tells us that our "research," rather than illuminating new data for us, simply hardens our biases and convictions. And so with shocking frequency, this result emerges from our "research":

Research does not expose the truth; it blinds us to it. Seek understanding but beware of research.

Data Misleads

An imaginary scene in Burbank, California, 1952.

Eight representatives are waiting patiently in a small room that has what they do not realize is a one-way mirror on one wall. Finally a young man arrives—the facilitator for their discussion. He engages them in some ice-breaking questions, then poses the question of that day:

"Imagine an enormous park. In the center, picture a four-story medieval castle with turrets, painted a soft blue. Leading up to the castle, imagine a wide street with stores on either side; imagine a perfect small American town in 1915—except that these stores are immaculate, freshly painted, and about two-thirds the size of a normal building.

"As you walk down the street, people in Goofy and Mickey Mouse costumes walk up to you and greet you happily. In various parts of the park, you find a ride through a jungle, a submarine trip, cars that race around a track, and other rides.

"Would you be interested in such a park?

"Would you fly two thousand miles to visit it?

"Would you pay a hundred dollars a day for your family to visit it?"

Almost certainly, the answers to those three questions would have been maybe, no, and absolutely not. And Disneyland and Disney World might never have been built.

This kind of research—the kind that asks the questions you might well ask—is plagued by three insurmountable problems.

First, the questions it asks are hypothetical, and

life is real. We spend our hypothetical time and money in a much different way than how we spend real time and money. What we actually do is often nothing like what we said we might do.

The second problem with "Would you like this?" research is that what you describe and what you deliver are not the same thing. The hypothetical Disney researcher's word picture, vivid though it was, couldn't adequately capture Uncle Walt's vision.

The final problem is the one this tale of Disney suggests most vividly. The more innovative your idea, the smaller the number of people who will understand it—and people have great trouble imagining that they will buy something they cannot understand.

Another example: Picture yourself trying to explain the personal computer and then asking your listeners if they would be interested in one. Only that tiny sliver of the population known as Innovators would say yes. Everyone else would say no. (In fact, in the early stages of most innovative products and services, almost everyone does say no, making "no" a not very meaningful survey answer.)

Even more important, the more innovative the idea, the more uncomfortable most people feel about it. Truly new ideas make people uneasy. When Fred Smith trotted his idea for Federal Express by his experienced and intelligent business professors, they thought it would never fly; Federal Express was too different.

You can see the pattern: The more innovative the idea, the less likely it is to survive this kind of scrutiny. And yet the more innovative the idea, the greater the potential success.

Research supports mediocre ideas and kills great ones.

The Case for Soft Evidence

The proposal to introduce healthy, low-calorie chicken at Kentucky Fried Chicken in the late 1990s has just been presented.

"Fine," the executive responds. "But where's the evidence?"

So the presenter offers some anecdotal—often called "soft"—evidence.

First, the presenter has just returned from a trip to Miami. On the flight down, he sat beside the director of food services for one of the world's leading cruise lines. After some nice ice-breaking, the food director revealed the American attitude toward food. "In America, it's all about quantity. Forget good. Give them plenty. Is it any wonder the French look like dancers and Americans look like Jabba the Hut?"

Second, the presenter notes that virtually everyone—even among the college-educated, most health-conscious portion of America's population—in every American restaurant orders the high-calorie items.

Third, the presenter mentions the January 3 Phenomenon. This is the annual explosion of health club attendance during the first full week after the Christmas holidays. By February 1, however, attendance is back to its quiet normal. All those newly committed health fanatics have abandoned their commitment and returned to lunch—a big, fried lunch.

That summarizes just some of the anecdotal evidence that would discourage a fast-food executive from introducing low-fat, low-calorie chicken.

Here was the hard evidence. The executives at KFC, like their counterparts at Pizza Hut and McDonald's, had commissioned exhaustive focus group studies, which seemed to offer incontrovertible evidence that people loved low-fat, low-calorie, skinless chicken, just as they said they liked low-fat pizza and the McLean sandwich. This "hard" research clearly showed that people would buy those items.

As the fast-food executive, which evidence do

you rely on? The hard evidence, of course. The anecdotes are mere stories. They are literature; the research is science.

As most readers have guessed, the product tanked. The executives had demonstrated an overlooked fact of marketing life: *Hard evidence is actually the worst evidence.*

Hard evidence is more dangerous because its apparent scientific-ness seduces people into relying on it. Executives then make decisions that common sense informed by anecdotal evidence would have talked them out of.

Anecdotal evidence is reliable because it emerges from the real world. Hard evidence emerges from artificial, laboratory situations such as focus groups. The Heisenberg principle reminds us that these laboratory situations are inherently flawed because people who are being observed change their behavior—and their opinions—as the result of being observed.

They do not give the answers that reflect their true opinions. They give the answers that reflect best on them—answers like "Yes, I do like healthy foods and would definitely buy these."

Ignore hard evidence. Soft evidence is much more reliable.

Lessons from Politics

One of the reasons "research" produces so much information of so little value can be found in the deep recesses of your own mind.

Do you know exactly who you are?

Do you know just what you would do in any given circumstance?

Do you always act consistently with your beliefs?

Do you do things that surprise you? That disappoint you? That you wish you hadn't?

Are you always the person you wish you could be?

The answer to all of these questions, of course, is no. And yet most market research assumes the answer to these questions is yes.

We want people to think we are health-conscious. So we tell researchers we would buy light burgers, light pizza, and light fried chicken. Then, as McDonald's, Pizza Hut, and KFC have learned, we don't.

In 1979, most people wanted others to think they were generous, liberal, and compassionate. So they told pollsters they were voting for the liberal candidate, Jimmy Carter, rather than that old friend of the rich, Ronald Reagan. And then they voted for Reagan: The voters told researchers one thing, then did another.

We do not know ourselves. We do not act as we think we might. We are often not the person we pretend to be, or want to be. And so we are not who the researchers think we are—and we do not do what research says we will.

Beware of research. People make terrible guinea pigs.

What Price Insight?

Working with a large West Coast–based retailer on a new name for its in-store services, the branding and naming firm finally had it—or so it hoped.

The firm's list was made up of six finalists, two semifinalists, and their winner: the name that met all their criteria for an outstanding name.

Rather than merely trust their judgment, however, the branding firm's executives called on a group of consumers to affirm it. The group was not representative; the thirteen consumers lived in a large Midwestern city, and had more education and earned far more than the retailer's prospects did. Nevertheless, the branding firm believed that this group was "normal" in statistical terms. Its responses to the name were likely to be very much like the bulk of responses in a truly representative sample.

The thirteen consumers agreed with the branding firm's recommendations, and gave their reasons why, as well as their reasons for not preferring the alternative names.

The retailer, however, had one other key audience to satisfy: its board of directors. The retailer's executives could not bring themselves to tell the board that they were recommending a multimillion-dollar name change on the basis of one measly thirteen-person focus group.

So the retailer commissioned a multi-state research project. Researchers interviewed over 350 people who matched the profile of its primary customers. The researchers reached a startling conclusion:

The same conclusion that the branding firm and its thirteen-person sample reached.

This finding merely confirms what marketing information-gatherers learn—or should. Five hundred people usually will lead you to the same conclusion that fifteen do. And, as necessary as they may be to placate boards of directors or to comfort top executives, large representative groups of "average" people do not offer particularly good information, because average people are only average. You do not want average information; you want exceptional insight.

Let's take a very specific professional service as an example: a sports medicine clinic. If you wanted to expand your sports medicine practice, whom should you talk to: hundreds of representative prospects—or a few uniquely insightful and influential ones? Let's say it's 1978, perhaps the peak of the running boom in America. Who could tell you the most that would help you the most?

It isn't the representative prospect on the street. It's the very influential top runners. They are true athletes, and therefore the most apt to use—and to need to use—sports medicine services. In addition, being committed—arguably, even fanatical—runners, they simply have thought more about the subject of their injuries and their frustrations with conventional treatments and conventional practitioners. They have studied the problem; in some cases, they have insights that the people operating the clinics do not.

Perhaps more important, these top runners are their market's Key Opinion Leaders. When these impossibly lean and improbably fast runners started wearing Casio watches and New Zealand split running shorts and rubbing Vaseline on their nipples before races longer than ten miles, the sales of all these products skyrocketed. The bulk of the market simply watched and followed the Key Opinion Leaders—as many markets do.

So at least two key principles emerge from the retailer's testing: (1) A little information-gathering will usually produce the same insights much faster and cheaper than an exhaustive study will. (2) Before you try to survey a representative sample, ask yourself: Just how valuable is *representative* information—isn't what you really need uniquely *insightful* information, from the people who lead the markets and influence them?

Beware who you survey—and how many.

The Second Twenty Minutes

A Fortune 500 company's CEO and I are chatting in a bar in Snowmass, Colorado. Our first twenty minutes proceed the way most ice-breakers proceed. We dance around some pleasantries, get comfortable, decide whether we should pursue a real conversation. Two glasses of scotch enter the frame, and are soon replaced by two more.

After about twenty minutes, the conversation changes. It deepens. And the depths it is heading for are the depths of real truth. At the outset, his sounded like just another successful and well-run company, growing nicely and pleasing its share-holders. But in time, we get to his reservations, his fears, his real view of his company and the market. We have moved beyond the press releases and the bluster, and have arrived, slowly and awkwardly, at the truth.

This exchange has significant implications for anyone who markets a service. This experience explains the best response to the question, "Where can we find the insights into this market that will help us make the best possible decisions?"

The best answer is, "In the second twenty minutes."

You find the key insights you need—after your own, which are the most critical—in the mind of your market's key observers and prospects. But they do not readily volunteer those insights. Often, they do not even arrive at them until they have entered a discussion in which they say one thing, then another, then piece the two together into something new. And they do not offer these easily—indeed, they rarely offer them at all—to someone they don't feel comfortable with.

During the first twenty minutes, these people have their guard and inhibitions up. Perhaps their biggest inhibition can be explained by a variation on the Heisenberg principle, the principle that says the mere fact of being observed changes behavior. A person being interviewed or sounded out feels exposed. The environment feels unnatural, the circumstances unusual; he feels pressured to perform, to sound intelligent, which in turn often creates the pressure to not say what he really thinks.

But people with some success in this kind of discussion notice a transformation over time. The subject gradually forgets the setting and her initial inhibitions, becomes more comfortable with her inquisitor and the topic. As ideas begin to form, she grows more interested in the ideas and more oblivious to the setting. And so, with time there is truth.

Organized research, or certainly formal research, will not help you arrive at these insights. You need conversations in which your subjects feel comfortable, in which they lose sight of the fact that this might be research.

Don't research; listen.

On the Outside Looking In

Professional outsiders offer at least one indispensable asset: their ignorance. They haven't yet learned what works in your business and what doesn't; why your business uses one set of processes and not another; or why you view turnover as good, for example, when someone with less information might think it's bad.

The contrast between the outsider and the insider, and the value of the outsider, reflects a basic truth: The closer we get to something, the less clearly we can see it.

An outsider holds the page at arm's length, and sees it as the market will see it. The letters get clearer. And the reader knows what he's reading, rather than what the author intended to convey.

We run our businesses as a succession of follies interrupted, we hope, by moments of brilliance or at least long stretches of competence. But in varying degrees, we do commit follies. We fail to see them because no one tells us, because we don't want to see them, and because business seems to be perking along.

Our greatest leverage lies not in polishing the areas where we shine most, but in addressing our areas of folly.

The story of the emperor's new clothes seems apt here. The emperor paraded naked through the streets, believing himself to be dressed in magical new finery, and no one said a thing. The town elders, experienced in these things and familiar with the ways of emperors, proclaimed the nonexistent clothes beautiful. Enter the most naive of them all, a young boy who had never observed emperors before. He saw no clothes at all—and said so. He reacted honestly because only he was uninhibited by experience and familiarity.

You need to take not just a wise look at your business, but a naive one. You want someone who will clearly see the folly that you and others too close to the business are missing. You need someone who sees what they truly see, instead of what they think you want them to see. You need to stop, pull back, look, and have an outsider help you look.

Find a boy to tell you what your emperor is wearing.

FALLACIES OF MARKETING

The Fallacy of Best Practices

When you walk into a clinic today, you feel confident you will walk out alive. You just don't know when.

You arrive at 9:28 for your 9:30 appointment, almost laughing at your needless punctuality. "Sure, my appointment is for 9:30, but I won't really see the doctor until 10, at least. What am I doing here?"

It's a good question. The health care industry follows the practice, "We will see you when we are ready."

The industry has set several other standards that you endure only because it has a virtual monopoly on your business.

If you come in for surgery on your arm, for example, you may be asked to sit around most of the day wearing a tiny cotton robe with no underwear underneath. You feel vulnerable and subservient. You feel awful. You may go through the pre-op procedures in one part of the building, then wait for a wheelchair or gurney to wheel you to another part—often, the other end of the hospital.

You find these practices at virtually every

American hospital and clinic. These are their "best practices." And this simple example demonstrates why entire service industries constantly disappoint and infuriate their customers.

Fortunately for the citizens of Salt Lake City, these practices also maddened two nurses, Diane Kelly and Joan Lelis. Kelly was a former neonatal-intensive-care nurse who decided to revolutionize health care by first returning to school for an MBA. When she returned to work at Latter-Day Saints Hospital, she articulated many of the changes she felt were necessary. Lelis, LDS's chief of surgical services, agreed and helped Kelly carry out the transformation. They added valet parking, offered hot blankets, enforced tighter adherence to schedules, mandated blood drawing during the inserts of IVs (to avoid a second puncture), and allowed ambulatory patients to walk rather than wait for wheelchairs.

At this point, a hard-bitten bean counter reader might suggest that these reforms probably increased patient satisfaction but reduced revenues. Hiring the valets and heating those blankets costs money, and while the other changes might have produced soft benefits, hard dollars were not among them.

That is not what happened at LDS, however. Studies showed that patients actually woke up feeling better, recovered faster, and returned home sooner. This increased the hospital's peak capacity more than 50 percent. LDS can now serve more patients in the same amount of space, thereby generating more revenue.

The LDS story has at least two significant messages for marketers. The first is that every service industry, including relatively mature ones like hospitals, can be dramatically reformed.

The second is that following industry standards or even best practices quickly becomes what no business can afford: an invitation to ordinariness. There is a hint of the problem in the verb itself: *following*. You don't want to follow, but to gain some competitive advantage. You want to lead.

Successful marketing hinges on creating distinctions; best practices quickly become common practices. Best practices also become a trap; you keep waiting for other practices to emulate rather than creating your own.

Ignore best practices. Then create them.

The Fallacy of Best Practices, Part 2: Nordstrom

Defying all convention, *Selling the Invisible* offered 250 pages about service without once mentioning Nordstrom.

Selling the Invisible ignored Nordstrom not because the very word has become a cliché in service, or because I was ignorant of the store. (Indeed, I bought my first pair of penny loafers at the Nordstrom's on Broadway Avenue in Portland, Oregon, in 1959.)

Selling the Invisible ignored Nordstrom because, Ross Perot's insistence to the contrary, businesses are not "just as simple as that." Too many people believe they can copy one of Nordstrom's practices and, from that, eventually duplicate the Seattle-based department store chain's success. Unfortunately for these optimists, businesses are complex systems. Various parts work in concert, each playing a role.

One example: Nordstrom commissions its salespeople. An executive at another chain learns this and decides to put his salespeople on commission, too. A year later, the executive happily notices a sales increase, and pats himself on the back. Six months after that, he begins noticing a significant exodus of new and older clients. He wonders why.

Often, the explanation for both phenomena—the sales increase and the subsequent loss of clients—is the same. The salesperson sold too hard, which got the sale but raised the buyer's expectations. The company could have met lower expectations, but failed to meet the higher ones. The clients became dissatisfied, and left.

Nordstrom does not succeed because of its sales commissions. It succeeds because it has created an entire system in which commissions work. In some systems, pure commissions work. In others, they will fail.

Don't copy. Your business is more complex than that.

The Fallacy of the Decision-Making Process

He was guilty, yet innocent.

This apparent contradiction perfectly describes two fallacies about the human decision-making process. The first is that decisions are *made;* and the second is that there is a *process*.

This romantic view of human behavior almost certainly dates to John Locke and the other eighteenth-century rationalists, who believe that man was a creature of reason and made decisions after weighing costs and benefits. With no intent of disparaging either side of this issue, however, let's consider the famous trial of O. J. Simpson.

Within days after Simpson was arrested in June 1994, two camps formed. The first camp, relying almost exclusively on Simpson's demeanor and the famous convoy he led in his white Bronco, decided he had killed his ex-wife and Ron Goldman. The second camp, relying primarily on impressions formed from seeing Simpson win Heisman trophies, give commentary on sports broadcasts, and act in movies, concluded he was innocent.

Three months later the trial began, and many months later, after hours of testimony and numerous witnesses, after commentators on every program from *MacNeil Lehrer* to *Entertainment Tonight* had dissected every shred of evidence, what had these people in each camp "decided"?

Nothing.

Those who before the trial had concluded Simpson was guilty still thought him guilty; those who proclaimed him innocent from the start still proclaimed him innocent. *Nothing had been decided.*

And what "process" had these people gone through? Certainly not a decision-making process; their decisions had already been made. Instead, they had looked at the evidence that supported their view, disregarded or explained away any contrary evidence, and offered their decision. They had not gone through this process to make a decision. They went through it to *justify* the decision they already had made.

Most decisions are not made; they are quickly reached, then justified.

We all do it. We do not seek enlightenment; we seek support for judgments we already have made, and in which we place remarkable faith.

We go "looking for cars," for example. We test drive several. Then we buy the car we subconsciously chose before the test.

We look for a new firm to outsource our payroll. We request and listen to presentations from several of the better-regarded firms. Then we choose the one we were going to choose anyway. We congratulate ourselves on gathering data and listening openly. But we have not listened openly; we have seen what we wanted to see, and have explained away anything that does not fit our prejudgments, biases, intuitions, and stereotypes.

As someone who markets a service, what can you do about this? Clearly, the first thing you need to figure out is what decision your prospect has already made.

In some cases, her decision in favor of a competitor may be so firm that your best tactic is to save your time, money, and effort and move on. In others, your tactic is to learn what basic "facts" she relied on in choosing your rival. In many cases, one or more of those facts is a misconception about either your service or the service she has picked.

Someone looking for consultants on systems integration, for example, might easily decide against the well-known consulting firm CSC, believing it to be primarily involved in reengineering or business strategy consulting, thanks to two best-selling books on those subjects by CSC Index employees. In fact, that person has it somewhat backwards. As the spelled-out name—Computer Sciences Corporation—suggests, CSC's historic strength has been in computer systems consulting. The CSC consultant would have been well advised to ask the question, "What do you know about us? What are our strengths that led you to invite us to talk with you?"

That discussion almost certainly would reveal the prospect's misconceptions, and help change her decision.

Before you try to influence a prospect's decision, find out what she's already decided—and why.

The Fallacy of Imagination

We value imagination in business, but barely understand it.

And our misunderstanding stifles our imagination.

We see imagination as the uncommon ability to create something totally new.

Test this definition against every creation that you consider imaginative, however, and what do you discover?

Totally new creations are not totally new after all.

As one vivid example, imagine American rock fans on April 12, 1965. That afternoon, in '56 Chevies at Coney Island, '64 Corvettes racing down the California coast, and everything in between, they first heard something utterly new: the Byrds' "Mr. Tambourine Man," with its riveting guitar line. The song immediately became part of the spirit of that summer, and that time. Millions bought the single and the album to keep it forever. We had never heard anything like it.

Or had we?

Consider the elements of the recording for a moment, and what those elements suggest about how we imagine, innovate, and create. First, the song itself wasn't created by the Byrds, but by the poet laureate of folk music, Bob Dylan. It was not, however, an obvious choice for a fledgling rock group. Its lyrics were far more esoteric and sophisticated than those of any Top 40 song of the day, and their implicit drug theme ("Take me for a trip upon your magic swirlin' ship") was forward-looking as well. Second, Roger McGuinn's ringing guitar, which creates the memorable intro, wasn't common in 1965, but McGuinn was not the first rock musician to use that particular guitar sound. Like almost every English-speaking person under the age of forty in 1965, McGuinn listened to the Beatles. And like every musician, McGuinn had good reason to listen intently: He wanted to figure out the Fab Four's secrets. One afternoon, he noticed a unique sound. It was George Harrison's guitar, and a sound McGuinn loved, but barely recognized.

What was that sound? McGuinn wondered.

McGuinn got his answer in a movie theater. There, watching the Beatles' *Hard Day's Night,* he spotted in Harrison's hands a very distinctive guitar: a Rickenbacker electric twelve-string. The next day, McGuinn rushed out and bought one—and "Mr. Tambourine Man" was on its way.

Third, McGuinn admired artists other than the Beatles. Like many early rock musicians, McGuinn trained in the classics. Listen to his arrangement of "Mr. Tambourine Man," and you can hear those roots. That arrangement echoes one of McGuinn's seminal influences: Bach.

Fourth, to serious students of music, McGuinn's genius was not in these elements, it was how he mixed them in the studio. Producer Terry Melcher and McGuinn mixed this song with another song in mind: The Beach Boys' "Don't Worry Baby."

Pick up a copy of "Don't Worry Baby" and listen. Now put on "Mr. Tambourine Man." You cannot miss the resemblance.

And so what was this remarkably innovative song? Like virtually all innovators, McGuinn did not create something utterly new. *He simply combined existing elements in ways no one had combined them before.*

The breakthroughs we salute and which often produce extraordinary returns for their "imagineers"—the personal computer, traveler's checks, and indexed mutual funds—never occur from nothing. The imagineer does not build by combining genius with air; she builds with existing ingredients. Breakthroughs—as McGuinn's recording illustrates—very rarely are original entities;* they are unprecedented *combinations*. Innovations combine things that have never been combined, often because no one believed the combination would work.

Take these three elements, for example: talk radio, information about cars, and the public-radio audience. What idiot would ever think to combine them? The idiots behind *Car Talk*, one of the last decade's most successful and innovative programs.

On close analysis, imagination is not a rare gift handed to a lucky few. We all own the building blocks for imagination—particularly if we look around and observe. The more we see, the more

*Occasionally, someone creates something the elements of which seem as original as the creation itself—Julie Taymor's remarkable staging of *The Lion King,* Jimi Hendrix's guitar playing, Orson Welles's production of *Citizen Kane,* and Wayne Gretzky's revolutionizing of offensive hockey, for example.

These creations cannot be satisfactorily explained, except to say that they are acts of rare genuine originality, produced by people who simply looked at what everyone else looked at and saw something different. In some of these cases, however, the artists have drawn on existing elements for inspiration. We simply cannot see it.

Anthony Hopkins's mesmerizing creation of the character Hannibal Lecter in *Silence of the Lambs* illustrates this perfectly. Lecter seems to resemble no screen character we have ever seen, until we learn the source of Hopkins's inspiration for the seemingly emotionless, amoral, and affectless Lecter: Hal, the talking computer in *2001: A Space Odyssey.*

we can combine—and the more "imaginative" we can be.

It's when we stop looking, learning, and growing that our work gets to seem too comfortable and familiar and stale. Singer-songwriter Paul Simon knows; he found himself in that imagination-free zone in the 1980s. Then he saw something utterly new to him: Africa.

Africa changed Paul Simon's "imagination." It upended his view of the world and of music, and led to his remarkably innovative album *Graceland*. Simon did not rediscover his creativity in Kenya and Somalia; he found new sources for combination.

He literally saw angels in African architecture; he felt a stranger; he found the ingredients to lyrics no one ever had written.

To imagine new and profitable ideas, we all must head for our Africas. We fertilize our imagination with learning. "Original ideas" spring fastest from well-furnished minds.

The North Carolina ad agency Long Haynes Carr Lintas realizes this. Each year it sends key staffers and clients for a four-day tour of New York at its most exotic. Everyone returns slightly charged, more imaginative. But their imaginations do not really change; they just discover things for their imaginations to play with.

To create more, learn something new.

The Fallacy of Leadership

"When all is said and done," someone once wrote, "more gets said than done."

Business books go on and on, filled with optimism and the implicit message, "It's as easy as this."

It's not.

John Lammers, an organizational development expert and professor at the University of California at Santa Barbara, expressed this when he proposed a sequel to *Selling the Invisible* called *Managing the Invisible*. Says Lammers, "Everyone wants to know, How do I get people to follow your advice—or anyone else's?"

How *do* you manage people to make these ideas work?

You don't.

Few Americans yearn to be managed; most talented people despise the very idea. You do not manage people. You create a business they care so much about that they don't require management; create goals so compelling that your employees manage themselves to achieve them.

In the last two decades, many prominent consultants have asked, "What makes great companies great?" While these books disagree on a few salient points, not one cites excellent managing as a significant influence.

With rare exceptions, extraordinary companies feel a compelling reason for being. Liberty Property Trust, a commercial real estate company based in Malvern, Pennsylvania, is obsessed with making each day of its tenants' lives a little better; Greene Espel, a Minneapolis law firm, with creating a community within its walls; Microsoft, with changing the world; Servicemaster, with doing God's work; Progressive, with revolutionizing insurance claims.

These obsessions drive the companies; employees need few directives, reminders, or motivational speeches. They organize around this compelling purpose—and work relentlessly to achieve it.

You can feel this quality in these companies' lobbies and see it in the people's walks. An outsider even learns its sound; where large groups of employees gather, the rooms echo with a low roar punctuated with frequent laughter.

The purpose leads the employees and, in many ways, manages them; it instructs them what to do. The purpose in turn imbues them with a spirit that attracts prospects and clients; the purpose becomes the centerpiece of the marketing. Employees and clients come—and stay.

How could they not?

People don't lead. Purposes do.

The Fallacy of the Ordinary Job

Consider the story that opens Daniel Goleman's best-seller, *Emotional Intelligence:*

One steamy August afternoon in New York City, Goleman boarded a bus on Madison Avenue, and immediately was startled. A cheery-looking fortyish driver welcomed him with a "Hi, how're ya doin'?", a greeting the driver repeated to each passenger who got on his bus as it slowly worked its way up Madison. In their equally steamy August moods, few people even acknowledged the driver's greeting. But slowly, what Goleman called "a magical transformation" took place. The driver gave a guided tour—describing a terrific sale at one store, a wonderful exhibit at a museum, and so on. Before long, the driver had altered the climate of the bus. The riders were transformed by his attitude, and they all smiled as they disembarked. Almost certainly, they carried the experience with them, perhaps well into the night.

The story exposes a weakness in most people's business thinking: the notion of the ordinary job. On its face, bus driving does sound like a fairly unremarkable job. Goleman's bus driver, however, saw it as more than getting people from point A to point B. Recognizing the job was only as ordinary as he allowed it to be, he decided to make it extraordinary, and did.

There are no ordinary jobs. There are only people who insist on performing them in ordinary ways.

The Fallacy of Novelty

"Familiarity breeds contempt." Like so many pithy expressions, this one sacrifices accuracy for brevity, the soul of an aphorism.

One can enjoy too much of any good thing, including familiarity. But we rarely make ourselves excessively familiar to clients and prospects; we're rarely familiar enough.

We limit ourselves if we fail to recognize not just the extraordinary marketing power in being known to a prospective buyer, but the liability in being little known—or not known at all.

Consider what appears to be a basic human instinct, acted out in several hundred wars over several thousand years. Strangers collide: the Indians and the settlers, the non-Greek-speaking outsiders and the Greeks. Do these strangers act with curiosity, or some slight attraction? Not at all. *Lack of familiarity breeds contempt.* Deep in our genetic code, an instruction warns us to treat the unfamiliar with suspicion. The unfamiliar is a threat we must avoid or overcome.

In this rather dangerous environment—the aptly named "pool" of prospects—what can we expect from prospects who are not already familiar with us? Politeness, perhaps—even to the point of her head apparently nodding in agreement when we first meet. But she has raised her defenses, appearances to the contrary. Her instinct is to repel us. Given our nature, we view other humans as predators. The prospect responds naturally; she avoids becoming our prey.

The meeting ends. Nothing happens; the prospect's name moves to our maybe file, then our year-old file, then our circular file.

What happened in that presentation—where did we go wrong?

We did not go wrong in the presentation. We went wrong *before* it. We failed to make ourselves familiar—and unfamiliarity breeds more than indifference.

It breeds contempt.

Before you try to sell yourself, make yourself familiar.

The Fallacy of the Obligatory RFP Response

We all wish we could be like Philip Johnson.

The story, apocryphal or not, is that a famous client sent Johnson's architectural firm a Request for Proposal, and in return received the shortest winning proposal in business history:

"I'll do it."

He did.

For all of us who are not internationally famous professionals, however, responding to RFPs is never this simple. The RFP process evokes images of Dante's circles of hell. Truly venal people are banished to a lower circle and damned to an eternity answering RFPs. (Soon, those responding imagine banishing to the hottest abyss the worst human being of all: the sadist who drafted that RFP.)

You can draft an answer almost as simple as Johnson's, however, and perhaps even as effective.

It is this written reply:

Because of the extraordinary demands for our service and the importance we attach to providing truly exceptional service to our loyal clients, we have a policy not to pursue (accounts/projects/ assignments) that require extensive proposals.

Our qualifications to perform the work you outline in your request can be found in the words of these loyal clients. We have included their names and phone numbers and have alerted them that you may be calling. These men and women would be happy to answer your questions and tell you why they chose us—and why they are elated they did.

We are eager to meet with you wherever and whenever you choose, to provide a detailed, concise, and clear description of how we would proceed with this work, and the costs, timetables, and other guarantees.

We are confident that like our clients, you and everyone at XYZ Corporation would be delighted with our work on this important task.

There are several reasons to adopt this tactic. Two stand out.

First, other than the government entities that are legally required to submit these detailed RFPs, the typical RFP comes from a client who often is simply shopping price—a client to be avoided.

Second, complying with the request costs far more than it appears. Entire teams put aside all critical tasks for valuable clients in order to locate boilerplate from other proposals, draft new sections, and argue which examples should be included. At least one staff person stays late printing and collating the weighty document. Ideally, several persons spend hours proofreading the documents in search of the tiny errors that can ruin the impression. People who could be warming up an excellent prospect devote days trying to win business that might not even be desirable: a client who will stay until he finds a better price.

One of America's best-regarded service firms recently reached the same conclusion. The company now has an informal policy that might be called "The Presumption Against RFPs." It presumes that any business that might come from an RFP is undesirable. Anyone who wants to pursue that client must overcome this presumption by showing why that client is desirable, and the effort of the proposal is justified. Otherwise, the company is wise to respond with three words:

We'll do it.

Before answering an RFP, make sure that you should.

The Fallacy of Competition

Who competes?

Does ADP? The outsourcing giant based in Atlanta appears to compete with Oracle and People-Soft. But it fights them with very soft gloves. To provide the service its clients need, ADP often must recommend and install Oracle and People-Soft software. For ADP to criticize these competitors is like a project manager at an architecture firm criticizing its own architects.

ADP needs these competitors as allies and partners. It cannot afford to criticize, insult, or alienate Oracle and PeopleSoft.

So the question truly becomes: Does ADP compete? And if so, with whom?

Greene Espel, a legendary litigation boutique in Minneapolis, specializes in several tight niches that involve complex lawsuits. With fewer than twenty lawyers on staff at this writing, the firm cannot handle all of a Fortune 500 client's legal work. What Greene Espel can handle, and regularly does, is complex *specialized* cases, particularly those filed in the upper Midwest. And where does the firm get many of these cases?

From large firms in Chicago, New York, and Minneapolis. Given that, can Greene Espel afford to appear to be competing with these firms for Fortune 500 clients? Not at all; it must—and does—make it clear that it wants to handle only those particular cases that fall into its "strike zone" of specialties.

Does Greene Espel compete? It does not. Like a species likely to endure for eons, it has found its place in the ecosystem where it can happily cooperate and still reap great rewards.

Institutional Venture Partners of Menlo Park, California, has emerged as one of the country's preeminent venture capital firms.* Like any great VC firm, it wants to attract the best clients by offering the most explosive possible ideas. But a venture capital firm very rarely provides most of a start-up's capital; the VC firm offers a portion and takes a stake, diversifying its investments like any good investor. The firm needs other skilled VC firms to provide capital, serve on the start-up's board, and good contacts in its own *keiretsu* (Silicon Valley speak for "network").

Does IVP compete? Do any venture capital firms truly compete?

Study the venture capital industry and you quickly learn that its prospects look to two sources for references on VC firms: other entrepreneurs, and the VC firms themselves. Given that, can IVP afford to compete explicitly against other venture capitalists and risk alienating them—and a rich source of references? Certainly not in classical terms; the firms fight, if at all, with light jabs and heavily padded gloves.

Who is your competition? In case after case, it is not other firms. You are competing with your prospect's view of your firm.

---

*The firm currently is morphing into two new entities, neither of which will use the IVP name.

We hear that in the world of business, dogs eat dogs, rats race rats, and only the strong last. Yet in case after case, we see that the strong did not claw their way up a competitor's back.

Instead, the two often grabbed hands and scaled the wall together.

Maybe you are not competing. Or maybe you shouldn't.

The Fallacy of Bundling

If offering one service is smart, bundling several together must be brilliant.

But does bundling work?

The flurry of financial mergers of the last decade spotlights this question. Citing "obvious synergies," a bank and an insurance company announce their marriage. The executives use "synergy" in two ways: as a euphemism for "firing all duplicative staff to reduce expenses," and as a signal to stockholders that they can now combine their services and products together in bundles, and sell even more. The more services you can offer, the reasoning goes, the more you *will* sell. This theory seems bulletproof, and immune to even devil's advocacy.

The devil, however, wins this argument. Bundling and its close relative, cross-selling, usually fail, for at least three reasons.

First, consider the force of habit. People behave habitually; we act as we always have, and change with difficulty, if at all. And so the personal banker becomes comfortable in her habits—selling mutual funds and similar investments to her client. Asked post-merger to sell or even recommend other options, she resists.

The banker has figured out mutual funds; she has not figured out variable annuities. She knows that a prospect always asks the one question a partly prepared salesperson cannot answer. Rather than risk her credibility with a client by revealing her ignorance, the personal banker—wisely— sticks with what she knows. She knows she can sell the mutual fund to that prospect anyway. She has no financial incentive to add to her bundle.

Finally, prospects prefer to work with apparent experts. The sheer complexity of items that can get thrown into a bundle (human resources compliance consulting, for example, often gets bundled into payroll processing) means that a salesperson must master two subjects rather than one. As offerings tend toward increased complexity—which they do, as illustrated by the existence of over 9,000 mutual funds today—only the remarkably gifted can master several subjects.

A bundle, however, forces the salesperson to represent herself as a Jill of several trades. This fights a basic human conviction: No person can master several trades. Michael Jordan dominated professional basketball; no one was surprised that he could not hit a curve ball.

Which brings us to the final reason bundling and cross-selling fail. Even if you build a relatively simple bundle, and even if the salesperson thoroughly understands and can clearly explain each part of the bundle, the bundle can still sink. The reason is that prospects do not buy what *they* do not comfortably understand. The more elements you add to a sale, the more you risk complicating the transaction, confusing the prospect, and killing the sale.

What is the bundler's alternative? Study the men and women who sell boats. They, to the dismay of extended-warranty providers, often resist even mentioning the extended warranty during the sale. The warranty providers argue that these sellers are just not very good, or hesitate for fear the price will look even higher. But these salespeople have learned on their feet what the advocates of bundling and cross-selling would learn, too:

The more you bundle into a sale, the more you risk losing the sale entirely.

Businesses today operate with a presumption

in favor of bundling. They see each customer as a distribution channel, and try to push several services through it. But the nature of the prospect suggests that we should begin with a presumption *against* bundling.

When in doubt, don't bundle.

The Fallacy of Assuming that Strategy Is Execution

"You hate Burger King," a reader of *Selling the Invisible* said. "But your precious McDonald's sure is in a mess."

Who could argue? McDonald's light meals have failed. The Arch Deluxe belly-flopped. The company's bewildering "55" campaign proved that the key to good promotions is making sure that people actually understand them.

At this writing, itchy McDonald's stockholders (who, for the record, include me) and students of marketing are watching for the company's next step. Many question whether the company's classic formula—cleanliness, speed, consistency—still works.

McDonald's problem, however, lies not in its

strategy, but in the execution. Consider the pillars on which McDonald's rests: cleanliness, speed, and utter consistency. And now, let's visit a typical McDonald's—the restaurant on Excelsior Boulevard in St. Louis Park, Minnesota.

Upon entering, you immediately notice several things you wouldn't have ten years before: several straw wrappers and ketchup packets on the floor. "If this is the restaurant," you worry, "what must the rest rooms look like?"

McDonald's is missing the "one that brung it." Its once spotless restaurants have grown spots. A typical store too often resembles the '50s hamburger joints that Ray Kroc drove from business.

McDonald's does not need a new strategy. It needs to execute its old one.

Another departure from the formula illustrates both the perils of success and a failure to adapt. In that same St. Louis Park McDonald's, a man can make a simple order of a McNuggets Happy Meal and a Super Size Quarter-Pounder and discover that it takes over three minutes to prepare and present his order. In 1970, guests might have accepted that wait, though it certainly was not common.

But in 2000, with life's pace quickened and the pace of many services keeping up, we no longer accept that three-minute wait. If a fax machine can send us a letter 2,500 miles in fifteen seconds, and a computer company can send us a $2,000 computer 1,500 miles while we are sleeping, we expect a "fast"-food restaurant to deliver a simple order in less than three minutes.

Our expectations have changed. McDonald's, alas, has not changed enough with them.

So McDonald's is also failing to execute part two of its formula for success: speed.

Obviously, the poor condition of this St. Louis Park store suggests that McDonald's is also struggling to maintain consistency. No longer could a hungry traveler feel confident zipping in to a McDonald's, knowing it would be a pleasant oasis. Maybe it would; maybe it wouldn't.

But the solution is simple enough: McDonald's must become McDonald's again.

Before you look at your marketing, look at your execution.

Pulverizing Your Competition with a Roll of Paper

"Point of difference" is marketers' jargon for the feature that distinguishes you from your competitors.

In creating the distinctions that can drive business, every marketer should think of point of difference in a new way.

Specifically, at what points do you make significant *contact* with prospects and clients? And how might you make it differently?

A points-of-contact exercise can facilitate this effort—and can also help you realize where your rubber meets the road.

To see what a POC exercise is about, let's eavesdrop on one done by about thirty members of the Southwestern Independent Booksellers' Association in 1998.

Step one: What are the points of contact between a bookstore and a customer?

You quickly realize this list is long. A partial list includes the bookstore exterior; parking (including convenience, comfort, and validation); accessibility; hours; signage; entrance; greeting; book products offered; nonbook products offered; amenities (free coffee, cookies, and others); shelving; payment and terms; printed information; personal advice; packaging; programs for frequent buyers; author events; nonauthor events.

Now, in column one, list what you are currently offering. Then list what your strong competitors are offering that is different and might be preferable. Then list the key items:

- What might you do?
- What is possible?
- What has no one done?

For starters, just focus on shelving. What if for your sports section you tracked down bleachers from an old ballpark and included with them a few stories on the great ball games in your town? Or you painted the kids' book shelving in bright colors and children's book themes? Or wallpapered the business section shelves in stock quotation paper?

Focus on advice. What if you called your most avid customers and asked them to recommend their ten favorite books in their favorite genre, and write a short review? Not only would you deepen your bond with those key customers, you would begin to make some of your customers more familiar with one another, which would enhance their experience of visiting the store.

What about packaging? What if you offered truly creative gift wrapping? The Minneapolis toy store Creative KidStuff turned its attention to just this small point of contact. The wizards at this growing group of stores make their packages almost as much fun as the toys they stock. (At this writing, Creative KidStuff is growing while Toys-R-Us is closing stores. Could Creative KidStuff have fought off its huge competitors with only a few spools of gift wrap? They could and they *did*.)

Inventory your points of contact. Then imagine what could make each one extraordinary.

When Butterflies Turn Ugly

It has happened to you. It is probably happening to your company.

You go to pay for an item from a well-known national retailer. Your checkout clerk seems indifferent and distracted. As it turns out, she is grousing with the clerk in the next lane about management—their new demand about proper work attire, let's say.

This simple episode affects you twice. It diminishes your satisfaction; the tone of the transaction clouds your experience. You hoped for a warm hello and equally warm goodbye. Instead, you got negativity.

Your other reaction damages the retailer even more. With relatively little data on which to base your sense of the company, your dominant impression becomes this one: Its employees are unhappy; maybe it's a bad company. You have not only been disappointed, but also have been led to believe you will suffer other bad experiences there. Almost without knowing why, you stop going there as often—or at all.

Experiences with services tend to be dramatic rather than incidental; brief encounters often have a far greater impact than you know. They have a Magnifier Effect: The effect of a contact is geometrically disproportionate to the event. The event was isolated, trivial, an instant snapshot in an epic movie. But the event becomes the entire story—the story your success hinges on.

We also see here the role of the Butterfly Effect, where the batting of a butterfly's tiny wings in Beijing causes a death from a hurricane in North Carolina next month. This effect dictates that the service provider must not merely look at the small stuff. The provider must recognize that because impact means everything, there is no such thing as small stuff.

Do more than watch the details; control them.

The Service Buyer's Curve

Buyer's of technological products can be described nicely by a bell-shaped curve. This curve also proves useful, if only for contrast, in the world of service marketing.

The technology adoption curve looks like this:

Innovators are the first people to buy a new technology. They love technology and pride themselves on being the first on the block to own something new. Innovators include the audiophiles who willingly endured long waits to get the first Carver receivers. And they are the car buffs who advance-ordered the first new Volkswagen bugs and Audi TTs.

In product markets, the existence of Innovators makes perfect sense. We understand the desire to be the first on your block, even if we rarely feel it. The Innovators buy a badge that says, I am an explorer, a groundbreaker, a very clever person. I run ahead of the field.

You may recognize how the technology product market—in fact, most product markets—differ from a service market. A service is invisible. Virtually no one knows and few care what services you use, with the exception of prestige services like country clubs, spas, and extravagantly priced restaurants. Your choice of accounting firm, dentist, dry cleaner, insurance company, and stockbroker is hidden from view; it rarely interests others. You cannot drive these relationships around your block, or show them off on your computer table.

Even more important, however, service buyers, with good reason, avoid risk. They know they can return a broken or failed product and get it replaced under warranty. And they typically have chosen the product after trying it out or on, for size, fit, function, and design.

But buying a service, by contrast, merely means buying some promise of future performance. The buyer knows she cannot turn the service back in. She knows that the quality of the performance of the service is largely a matter for debate.

For this reason, whereas the first stage of a product market has a nice sample—8 to 10 percent—of Innovators, the typical service opens its doors on a much different market. No one wants to be the first on his block to try a new service. Instead, this tiny segment—exceedingly tiny—can best be described as friends, family, and bottom feeders—the latter being the people who buy the low-priced service, which a new service often is willing and even forced to be. These are the people within the founders' circle whom they carefully round up before they open their doors. For this reason, entrepreneurs are often pleasantly surprised by first-quarter sales. Thanks to their friends and family, and a few nice referrals here and there among them, business often opens briskly.

Then reality hits.

And the reality is this: The heart of your market is miles away.

Beware of early success. Your buyers are far down the bell-shaped curve.

The Fallacy of the Virtual Alternative

It was the perfect Web marketer. If any company could market itself on the Internet, this one could.

It was a Midwestern telephonic software company. Its target audience was perfect for Web marketing: technologically inclined employees, usually working in an information systems capacity. Virtually every key prospect for this company's product surfed the Web.

Not surprisingly, the company quickly established a Website. The site was competently done, clearly written, and pleasantly free of those maddening images that take forever to download. After nine months, this company—the perfect Internet marketer—tallied its initial results.

Nothing. To be fair, one somewhat qualified prospect inquired. But he ultimately disappeared. Nine months, one lead, no sales.

At least temporarily, the thousands of companies that fear they are losing business by not having a Website can breathe easier. Amazon.com has obviously demonstrated that you can sell products at a discount on the Internet, but it has not yet proved you can make a profit doing so, and selling products at a discount is much different than offering a service.

Competitiveness and technology anxiety still prompt many companies to invest in a Website and it may still pay off. That, in fact, is the best current reason to explore technology: to become more conversant with the tools that might make a difference one day. "E commerce," for most service companies, represents a training investment, not a marketing one.

The service business considering this investment, however, should be wary. If the initial investment of time and money looks questionable, wait, because your real losses almost certainly will be greater.

Technology may one day help you, but your real marketing needs are more fundamental—service, brand, packaging. *Fix your fundamentals first.*

We have all heard the prophecy. "Once we delivered products and services face to face," the experts suggest. "Now we will deliver them electronically.

"An electronic 'person' will take your order, deliver what you request, and spare you the inconvenience of getting in your car, driving someplace, and jostling with other shoppers."

The words of these prophets, it seems, should be written on the subway walls. They are not prophecies; they are graffiti written by those whose lives depend on predicting radical change.

Pause for a moment, and consider. You have heard that Internet prophet's thinking before; by changing a few nouns, we have the predictions of just a few years ago: the predictions that people would stay home, ogle catalogs, order the coveted merchandise over the phone, and have it delivered to their door. Faster, better, perhaps even cheaper, if you calculate the money value of time and the cost of driving a car.

But what have the catalogs done to stay alive, and grow?

They have opened—could it be possible?—*stores*. Where once Eddie Bauer, J. Crew, Pottery Barn, Banana Republic, and dozens of others existed mainly as names on warehouses and return addresses, now they fill malls and mini-malls everywhere.

At this writing, catalog sales sit 20 percent below their very modest goals for Christmas, and their company stocks are falling with them.

Granted, the problem for Lands' End, for example, also included too much inventory. But inventory did not precipitate the industry-wide slump; the concept did. The obvious theoretical appeal of catalogs—and even their great emotional appeal, captured so well by Roger Horchow in his wonderful book *Elephants in Your Mailbox*—is *too* theoretical. It presumes we are creatures of convenience. It also fails to realize that even the introverts among us are social; we are social animals who have always depended on one another for our very survival. We go out just to go out.

We shop just to be among strangers; we dine out just to people-watch. We continue to attend movies in enormous numbers when our DVDs and thirty-six-inch Surround Sound sit waiting to deliver entertainment to us in our cocoons.

A cyber world may be coming. But no evidence supports that we are cybers.

We are social. As proof, the worst form of punishment we inflict on someone who has broken our laws, short of taking his life, is to lock him up alone in a cell and not let him mix with others. If a prisoner misbehaves, how is he punished? With *solitary* confinement—being left truly alone.

We do the same to our children when they are bad; we give them time-outs and make them spend that time alone.

What does this tell us about where we are going, and where you should take your business?

You should take it to people, and keep it there. Make real connections. In the apt and succinct words of N.W. Ayer:

Make human contact.

WHAT IS SATISFACTION?

If They're Satisfied, You're Doomed

The absurdity of striving for customer "satisfaction" can be illustrated by a story from the speaking industry.

One very early morning in her office in Redmond, Washington, Roxanna Frost is struck with an idea. "Maybe I should have Harry Beckwith come speak about marketing. I wonder if his speeches are as good as his book?"*

Roxanna calls Chicago, where Rick Salzer, a vice president for marketing with a Fortune 500 company, is plotting the demise of his competitors.

"Rick, Roxanna Frost from Microsoft. We're thinking about having Harry Beckwith come speak here. How did you feel about his presentation to your company?"

Imagine how Roxanna reacts if Rick answers:

"We were *satisfied*."

Would Roxanna hire the speaker based on that lukewarm recommendation? No.

---

*This story has been changed slightly, to avoid the appearance of self-promotion. Rick Salzer actually loved the speech, and Roxanna hired me, for which I thank her again.

Prospects hope to be *at least* satisfied. As this conversation reveals, "satisfied" clients do not help your business, and "very satisfied" clients help only a little. (Imagine the effect of Salzer saying "We were very satisfied.") You want surprised and delighted customers; you want customers who will not simply offer nice references, but volunteer them; clients who do not simply respond to your service, but take time from their busy lives to write and thank you for it.

If your goal is satisfied clients, your goal is far too modest.

The Surprise at General Motors

Like many American automobile manufacturers in the mid-1980s, General Motors got the quality religion most famously expressed in Ford's then-new chant, "Quality is Job One." Like Ford, General Motors improved the quality of its cars. Like Ford, General Motors surveyed its customers, and learned that they were far more satisfied than they had been before the quality initiative. Ninety percent of them were, in fact.

And then something funny happened. Those "satisfied" and even "very satisfied" General Motors customers went out and bought Toyotas, Hondas, and Fords; fewer than half of the satisfied customers bought the same GM make again. General Motors' market share and profits declined.

Client satisfaction is almost meaningless; measuring it will tell you very little, except that your percentage of satisfied customers is either going up or down—something you can figure out on your own from listening carefully. Client and customer expectations are constantly increasing, and your competitors are almost certainly improving, or trying to. You must get better just to stay even.

Stop measuring client satisfaction and start increasing it.

The Second Law of Satisfaction Dynamics

What makes satisfying clients so hard?

The psychologist Abraham Maslow provided a good first answer.

Maslow is best known for his hierarchy of human needs, from the basics of food and shelter up to the need for self-actualization. By identifying and ranking these needs, Maslow gave to six generations of marketers worldwide both a perspective and a common vocabulary for understanding and appealing to people.

Another insight of Maslow's, however, seems to have gone unnoticed, but it is a valuable one. "The human animal," he wrote, "is incapable of being satisfied except for brief moments. Once satisfied, he moves to his next need to be filled."

You might briefly notice that this human trait—which you almost certainly share—is both a weakness and a strength. Our tendency to be dissatisfied with the way things are drives us to improve them. It's the spur that led Renoir to paint extraordinary canvases, Frank Gehry to design his extraordinary museum in Bilbao, and Julie Taymor to create her remarkable staging for the musical *The Lion King*.

Unfortunately, human restlessness—and therefore, client restlessness—makes the task of satisfying people very difficult. Let's quickly examine one of the ironies that makes this so.

You land the account and win the client over. You begin working with her. At some point early in the relationship, someone in your company does something special to help her. What happens?

Your client feels good for some time. But your good deed also affects her expectations. Your good deed shows what you are capable of. With that, your client's expectations of you increase. From this moment forward, you must perform slightly better to meet her increased expectations—and significantly better to exceed them. Now, given that merely meeting a client's expectations is not quite enough, the irony becomes obvious: The better you do, the better you must do next time.

The American hotel industry is just recognizing this Escalating Expectations Syndrome. For their more frequent guests, many hotels have created so-called club floors with special services. But what happens when even that is not enough?

Consider the California hotel that completely redecorated a room for one of its more frequent guests. How does that guest feel now? a newspaper reporter asked. She discovered that Maslow was absolutely right.

"I expect even more than I used to," the guest admitted.

In the words of the old song, "How ya gonna keep 'em down on the farm, after they've seen Paree?" But the challenge in satisfying people doesn't stop there.

How do you satisfy them with Paris—*once they've seen Paris?*

How do you satisfy a client with "great," once you've already delivered it?

You must get better to avoid falling behind.

Perception Is Reality

The purist and the professional share a dangerous blind faith.

They believe that if they perform their service well—professionally, in the professional's jargon—the world will notice and reward them.

This faith may reflect the nineteenth-century conviction that people are rational and discriminating. We are *Homo sapiens:* wise human beings. Perhaps we are wise; it does not matter. We perceive badly.

Remember the balding man who rubbed a lotion into his scalp, thinking it was Rogaine, and weeks later, he saw new hairs on his head? There were no new hairs; that lotion was a placebo. He was in the control group for the market test.

We see what we want to see.

Another example. Poison ivy causes rashes. But what would happen if you exposed people to a plant that *looked* like poison ivy and told them it *was* poison ivy?

Logic answers, "Nothing." A harmless plant will not suddenly cause itching blisters simply because someone calls it poison ivy.

But a Japanese study showed just the opposite: People exposed to fake poison ivy develop real rashes. Cognitive neuropsychologists explain this with what they call "expectancy theory."

Expectancy theory is simply this: If your mind expects something to happen, it will. If you expect a rash from a plant or pain relief from a pill, you actually will get it.

Some doctors in Texas demonstrated this power of mind over body—and ultimately *on* the body—by operating on two groups of patients who had swelling and knee pain. In group one, they simply cut three holes in the patients' knees, then pretended they were operating.

In group two, the doctors scraped out the knee joints, a proven procedure for alleviating pain and swelling.

What happened? The phony procedure worked as well as the proven one. The two groups reported equal reductions in pain and swelling.

We experience what we believe we will experience. This means that anything and everything a service can do to *convey* quality, expertise, and the ability to perform well likely will enhance client satisfaction. *Conveying* quality can be as critical to satisfaction as actually delivering quality.

The issue for the purist and the professional is not whether their service is so good that the client *should* feel satisfied. The issue is, *does* your client feel satisfied, and does that feeling persist?

Put another way: On the subject of satisfaction, the client's perception is always right.

Your job is not to deliver a service; it is to create satisfaction.

Make your clients believe they will be satisfied, and they will be, especially if you do it with passion.

THE FIRST KEY:
PRICE

The More It Costs, the Better It Seems

In the spring of 1980 you are watching television, and it appears: the marketing event of your lifetime.

The commercial is shot in black and white, apparently on location. The announcer begins to talk quietly, almost in a whisper.

"Ladies and gentlemen, tonight we are at the fabulous San Francisco dining spot the Blue Fox. Tonight's diners have just sampled a wonderful meal, and are finishing their coffee." Then his voice turns more solemn and dramatic.

"And what they don't know," he whispers, "is that the coffee they are drinking is Folgers Crystals.

"Let's talk to one of the guests, and see what she thinks."

Naturally, she loves her coffee. *"Fabulous,"* she says.

"Well," the announcer responds, "would it surprise you if I told you it was *Folgers Crystals?"*

Why yes, it would, she says.

What just happened to that woman? Why did she love freeze-dried coffee?

The assumption drives the experience. You

don't taste the coffee; you taste your assumption. The coffee does taste great.

Even though it doesn't.

Price is more than the quid pro quo for the service you provide. Like money, price talks. It changes perceptions.

Price communicates the quality that purchasers can expect: We expect a high-priced item to perform very well. But price does more than just communicate. As the diner at the Blue Fox demonstrated, a high price can convince us that something we have experienced, even something clearly inferior in quality, was actually very good.

Price does not merely change assumptions and perceptions. Price changes the actual experience of using the service: *A high price actually improves the experience.*

Bear in mind an additional meaningful lesson from this commercial. The Blue Fox was selling coffee. Coffee has several physical characteristics: color, aroma, body, flavor, acidity, and others. We can subject coffee to our senses, and evaluate it objectively. Thus it should be relatively hard to fool a coffee drinker into believing artificial coffee is excellent.

But contrast this with services such as legal and accounting services, industrial psychological consulting, remote network management, tutoring, and thousands more. What objective and tangible features can a client use to decide those services are adequate, much less excellent? With fewer objective and tangible characteristics to assess, the user of these services is even *more* vulnerable to strange influences—like that of price—than the Folgers coffee drinker is.

The price of a service influences what the prospect expects, and what the client perceives—and experiences. Price helps create the rose-colored glasses through which people view a service. We may appreciate a low price; it may represent all we can afford. But while we may welcome the savings and recognize the service's "good value," we do not appreciate its quality; we assume we could do better.

And if and when we can afford it, we do.

Watch what your price says.

THE FIVE-DOLLAR SHAKE

Cut to *Pulp Fiction:* The characters played by Uma Thurman and John Travolta are sitting in a booth at a glitzy '50s-style diner/dance club, pondering their menus. Travolta orders a steak and a vanilla Coke. Thurman orders a burger . . . "and the Five-Dollar Shake."

Travolta, incredulous, asks her, "Did you just

order a five-dollar shake? That's a shake—that's milk and ice cream?"

"Last I heard," Thurman coolly replies.

He asks the waiter, "You don't put bourbon in it or nothin'?"

"No."

Travolta appears satisfied with this answer as the waiter walks away. When the waiter returns with the vanilla Coke and the Five-Dollar Shake, Thurman sucks languidly on her straw and Travolta says, "You think I could have a sip of that?"

Travolta has exposed a flaw in the marketing textbooks. They refer constantly to price resistance, but price resistance in those texts mean resistance to high prices. What is Travolta doing?

He is showing he is *attracted* to high prices.

Travolta never would have asked to try the Two-Dollar Shake; he would have resisted it. But he had to try the Five-Dollar Shake; he could not resist.

Push price higher. Higher prices don't just talk; they tempt.

THE DUCK AT TURTLE CREEK

My mother, Alice, had a special talent. Anything that my father could kill with a rifle, my mother could transform into something delicious. Even the renowned chef James Beard once admired my mother's wizardry in the kitchen. But Beard, poor man, never sampled Mom's delicious duck. (The secret, for you chefs: endless marinating.)

As the son of a world-class cook, I had spent many an afternoon at our kitchen table reading Mom's *Gourmet*s and *Bon Appetit*s and learning the differences between hollandaise and bechamel, mincing and chopping. And from those magazines I learned about a spectacular Dallas eatery called the Restaurant at the Mansion on Turtle Creek.

So it was that when I flew into Dallas for the first time in May 1984, I made a beeline to the Mansion for dinner. I ordered the duck. Aware of the enormous price of each bite, I ate very, very slowly. The duck tasted just as I thought it would, given all that I had read about the restaurant: exceptional. And for years, that is how I remembered it.

But beginning a few years ago, when I started to consider the bewildering lessons of service marketing, I have compared that duck with my mom's. Without denying that the Mansion serves very good food, I am now convinced that their braised duck was only good, not exceptional. But only someone with years of experience eating extraordinary duck—someone like the son of Alice Beckwith—would know this.

With rare exceptions like this one, we cannot easily differentiate the real technical quality of a service: the true value of a chef's food, a consultant's advice, or an architect's design. Our inability to distinguish quality leaves us enormously susceptible to other cues about a service's quality—and a service's price provides one of those few cues.

A price tells us how good a service probably is, then convinces us how good the service probably was. And so it is that we think duck that costs nearly as much as diamonds tastes delectable— even when it doesn't.

Price creates perceptions, then creates satisfaction.

THE AMAZING CASE
OF THE GIBSON GUITAR

The reader who fears that John Travolta and Uma Thurman merely illustrate the odd behavior that characterizes all Quentin Tarantino films should consider this remarkable tale.

For eons, Gibson had made legendary guitars. It pioneered the electric guitar, including the famous Les Paul Custom, and every serious guitarist has noticed that Eric Clapton often uses a Gibson. But with the growth of guitar-based rock and popular music in the 1960s came a flood of competition, particularly from Japanese manufacturers. By the mid-1980s, the legendary guitar maker was on the verge of becoming just a legend.

Gibson's obvious solution could be found in its problem: The Japanese had entered the guitar market with the same strategy their countrymen had followed in the automobile market: offering well-made, defect-free, highly competitive performance at significantly lower prices. Gibson's counterattack seemed obvious: Lower its prices so that its guitars were more competitive. Clearly, all those new owners of Japanese guitars were sending a clear signal that guitar buyers were sensitive to higher prices. At worst, Gibson's executives reasoned, they would increase volume of units sold and stabilize their market share.

What happened? Gibson's price reductions did not increase its unit sales. The price reductions actually led to fewer units sold. The classic law of price and demand—reducing prices increases demand, and vice versa—simply did not apply!

When it became clear that lower prices were further threatening the survival of the company, Gibson abandoned the reductions. It *increased* the price.

You've probably guessed what happened.

Demand increased. In fact, the more Gibson increased its prices, the more guitars it sold.

Faced with two identical services, one relatively low-priced and the other relatively high-priced, the person who can reasonably afford either service often chooses the higher-priced service—often for no other reason than its high price.

Increasing your price, in other words, will not necessarily decrease your volume, any more than decreasing it will increase your volume. Like so many tactics in marketing, these pricing tactics often have the opposite of their expected effect.

The higher your price, the higher your perceived quality.

How to Attract the Wrong Clients

Your ace salesperson returns to your office with a new account.

"I gave them a little discount, but I think it will be worthwhile."

Chances are, she thinks wrong.

Discount customers shop for discounts, and they can always find another discount and a lower price than yours.

Discount customers come and go. They are

more likely to appear in red ink than black; your hidden costs of acquiring and serving them as clients probably exceeded what they paid you.

Discount customers refer no one to you; they don't stay long enough to form an impression—and they are not very good judges of quality anyway. If they were, they would know that most economies are false ones, and that few service providers are low-cost providers by choice.

Discount customers are not your business; at best, they are cash flow. But most likely, they are a cost that you do not need and should not incur.

The discount client is not buying you, or the quality of your work, or her regard for you and your service. She is buying your price tag. She is not loyal to people and companies; she is loyal to price tags. You cannot build a lasting business on discount shoppers, and you cannot build a satisfying business and experience with them, either, because they do not value you and your work. In fact, in their continual efforts to get you to charge less, they are vividly communicating to you that your work is not worth to them what it is to you. You do not want or need these customers, and yet service businesses take them on by the millions every day. And then they wonder why their work—never mind their income—is not more satisfying.

Avoid the discount buyer.

IF THEY COME FOR THE PRICE, THEY'LL LEAVE FOR THE PRICE

In 1995, it appeared that Boston Market could do no wrong.

As if from eggs hatched overnight along America's major roads, these restaurants suddenly appeared everywhere, and everyone seemed to be buying their fast and remarkably inexpensive food. Everyone seemed to be buying their increasingly expensive stock, too. It soared to over $41 a share on December 4, 1996.

Then the sky fell. The stock hit $15.25 in just six months. Eighteen months later, on New Year's Eve, 1998, you could buy a share of Boston Chicken, the chain's parent company, for 33 cents.

What happened?

Overexpansion, it appears—and analysts typically mention that sin first when they describe the company's descent into Chapter 11. But the parent company also believed the old saw, "Come for the price, you'll stay for the food." They mailed millions of discount coupons in 1996. The offer, it turned out, worked like a bad charm.

Far more people than anyone expected redeemed the coupons. This created long lines, which in turn slowed the service, overcrowded the restaurants, and amplified the decibel levels.

The result: uncomfortable, noisy, messy restaurants. The coupon strategy is "Try us, you'll like us." But if everyone tries a restaurant on the same day, no one will like it.

Perhaps worse, those lines were filled with the wrong customers: price shoppers. By definition, price shoppers simply do not come for the price, then stay for the food. They come for the price. When another restaurant offers them a better price, they leave you. Exactly that happened.

Months later, recognizing they had gone too far with the coupons, the company scaled them back. In August 1997, they eliminated them completely. The price shoppers, disappointed, fled. The people who liked the food and might have liked the new ambience remembered the crowds and the noise and never returned.

And Boston Markets may never return from Chapter 11, either.

If people come for your price, they will leave for someone else's.

BUT WHAT ABOUT WAL-MART?

Sam Walton died rich, looking smart.

His success with Wal-Mart makes a discount strategy look smart. But while this strategy can work, it almost always fails.

You can spot the very weakness of a pricing strategy in the colorful description of companies like Wal-Mart. They're called "category killers." Months after Wal-Mart posts its Grand Opening banner, its competitors post theirs: Going Out of Business.

Wal-Mart deserves its success; the company is truly rare. But for every Wal-Mart that succeeded, a hundred chains that stressed low price failed. Witness the recent disappearance of Montgomery Ward, Janeway, Caldors, and Woolworths and thousands of local retailers.

One lives. One hundred die.

Categories don't get killed; companies do.

And the price-off providers usually die first.

The low price position kills.

The Two-Dollar Excuse

"We're getting killed on price. The market is very price-sensitive."

Maybe it is. But often, it isn't.

Among our first clients was a company that created the film master for bar codes that are used for printing them on packages. At our first meeting we asked them why they had lost business.

Their response—the overwhelming favorite response of all businesses to this question—was simple: "We're losing on price."

We asked the director of sales if we could contact their last twelve prospects who chose a competitor instead, to find out why. We did not ask them whether they rejected our client on price. Instead, we asked them, "What price range do you expect to pay for this product?"

They said they expected to pay from $8 to $10. That was the price they considered good, affordable, and fair.

Our client, who was supposedly losing these people because it was charging them too much, was quoting a price of $8.50—below the midrange of what the prospects expected to pay!

These prospects clearly were not rejecting our client based on price. But saying "It was price" is the easiest excuse—and one of business's great white lies.

It is far easier to say "You cost a little more than we wanted to pay" than "We really didn't think your quality equaled that of Brand X" or—the most common reason for rejecting a service—"We just didn't like you that much. We liked the other guys more."

Price is often the excuse for why you lost, but rarely the reason. Look deeper.

SALES, NOT PRICES

We're losing on price, you hear again.

But in most services, there is no clear "right price" for the service. People have a well-developed sense of what shoes, ties, cappuccinos, and cars cost. But what should a remodeled kitchen cost? And what should the architect cost? The true answer depends on what value he gives for the price that he charges.

Expressed in another, simple formula, this is how pricing works in service:

Apparent perceived value of service - Price = Value

Your quoted price may be more money than the prospect has, so she literally cannot afford your price. But most people who can afford the low price have the resources to pay far more. They refuse to pay far more for your service not because of its price, but because of its apparent perceived value. You have failed to create in their minds "apparent perceived value for the service." You have failed to convey any more apparent perceived value than the service that charges 30 percent less. So the prospect opts to pay 30 percent less.

Your problem was not your pricing; it was your selling.

Don't charge less. Sell better.

The Problem of the Hourly Fee

Jean Griffin contacted a well-known Chicago family-law attorney for help with her divorce.

The attorney described what is perhaps the most ludicrous and yet most common practice in all of professional services: the hourly fee. The attorney would charge Jean for the hours he spent on her divorce; the more hours he spent, the more she would have to pay.

Lawyers, most consulting practices, advertisers, architects, and dozens of other service businesses follow this practice. It is standard.

It is also absurd—a classic case of "client blindness."

To fully appreciate why, put yourself in Jean's shoes. Jean wants a fair and speedy resolution of her conflict for a fair price. And like the buyer of any other product or service, she also would like to know how much she'll have to pay for it.

The standard practice of hourly fees not only fails to answer any of these needs, *it actually works against them.*

What an hourly fee really says, almost comically, is this: The longer you must wait, the more

91

you must pay. Longer is bad enough; but longer and costlier is terrifying.

In legal and other practices, hourly fees clearly incentivize delays, attenuate deliveries, and encourage make work. And they clearly penalize the expert who can solve the problem quickly.

An advertising legend started his own business, and at one of his first client meetings, figured out the entire campaign and accompanying copy within fifteen minutes of the client's opening remarks. The legend, following customary practice, now had a crisis.

Did he bill these people $45 for his time—a fairly generous $180 per hour?

Of course not. That would penalize genius and efficiency. So instead, the ad business and other industries penalize their clients for their inefficiencies, and demonstrate a classic business problem: We do not follow our client's wishes; we follow our own industry's common—and often utterly unjustifiable and very annoying—practices.

Charge by your worth, not by the hour.

Tiered Pricing

At dozens of corporate events throughout the world this year, sales, marketing, and customer service people are asking the question.

How much service is too much?

Librarians at Microsoft, for example, wonder how they can honor some employees' requests for hours of assistance when Microsoft employees outnumber the library's staff by 500 to 1.

Family-law specialists ask how they can serve distraught clients who can easily spend hours on the phone discussing their psychological trauma, a problem the lawyer cannot professionally address, much less solve.

Recently, computer service firms like ADP have asked a similar question—and devised the preferred solution.

ADP realized that different clients want different levels of service. Some clients want "24x7": service any hour of any day. Some hotel clients want the turndown at night, chocolates on their pillow, and the *Wall Street Journal,* the *New York Times,* and two local papers in the morning. Others just want a TV.

Because clients are different, ADP offers Platinum, Gold, and Silver service packages. The client who wants a little more pays a little more.

ADP's solution seems obvious. Yet few companies have thought to create tiered pricing.

Build choices into your pricing, too. Think about it.

THE SECOND KEY: BRAND

Back to the Blue Fox

Let's return to the Blue Fox (page 77), and to our guest delighted with her coffee.

The high price for the coffee subtly influenced the woman to believe that her coffee, far from having been frozen, dried, artificially preserved, stuffed into a glass jar, and sold at a discount, was the finest fresh-brewed. But one more powerful force was working on her.

All the restaurants in which the Folgers commercials were filmed had one thing in common: Their reputations preceded them. The guests caught in the act of savoring their cups of instant coffee all had to be aware of the high status of these fabled restaurants. Many of the guests had read about these restaurants in *Gourmet,* the *New Yorker, Sunset,* and other glossy magazines.

As a result, these people did not merely assume they would be served great coffee in these restaurants; they *knew* they would. And so they sipped the coffee, and it tasted fabulous—*even though it didn't.* They had already made up their minds.

Brands do that. They attract people, bias people, and convince them that qualities that are missing are present. Brands play an enormous role in the marketing of services—as the following stories detail.

How to Double Your Fees Overnight

A consultant with an excellent but virtually unknown New York consulting firm arrived at David Schlossberg's office in New Jersey one day, offering his services to David's firm. David was impressed with the consultant's presentation, which addressed the firm's critical need for tax consulting. David, however, was concerned about the consultant's price, which was $1,250 a day.

Within two weeks, the consultant had taken a job with a Big Six firm in New York. A week after taking the job, the consultant approached David Schlossberg again. David asked how much the consultant was charging.

"Twenty-five hundred dollars a day," the consultant answered.

They signed an agreement that morning.*

---

*This story was related to me twice by an executive of IMI, the staffing and consulting firm. Experience convinces me it is true.

In three weeks, the consultant's market value had doubled. He had acquired no new skills and only fifteen working days of additional knowledge. He had done nothing to increase his real value; he had, however, dramatically increased both his perceived value and his price by simply acquiring a brand.

Acquire, build, or align yourself with a brand.

You Are Coke

Twenty-four out of twenty-five American businesses ignore branding. In some industries—arbitration, law, and vocational education, to name just three—the very idea of a brand is absurd. "We are not Coca-Cola," the executives of these businesses contend, and go off to concentrate on matters they consider more important.

But they miss the fundamental point. You do not choose to have a brand. You have one. Perhaps you think of it as your reputation, but it is a brand: it comprises everything your name evokes in your market.

The question is, are you going to seize that brand, manage it, nurture it, and realize its extraordinary potential—as Yahoo!, for example, has done—or are you going to allow it to seize you?

Carpe brand. Seize your brand.

The Wizard's Just a Little Old Man

When marketing experts preach "branding," most listeners hear "spin." They envision agencies and design firms crafting slick images to do what the Wizard of Oz did by projecting his outsize image on the drapes: persuade people he was something he was not.

The great brands do no such thing. Indeed, the great brands endure because both their presentation and their service delivery support their message. Of this there is no better example than the State Farm insurance company.

In its marketing communications, State Farm is dependability personified. Its jingle says it all: "And like a good neighbor/State Farm is there." There is no rock, no skyscraper, no tricks or mirrors. Historically the company's advertising falls so short of Hollywood production values as to seem almost like home movies.

But it works. State Farm's presentation works because it matches its performance. Customers find that time after time, State Farm really "is there"—a theme that conveys a compelling and simple promise. In fact, when Hurricane Andrew pummeled South Florida in 1992 one of the few pieces of good news to come out of that disaster was State Farm's response. Just as it promised, State Farm was there, quickly—with one employee for every eight Florida claimants, often overpaying claims to expedite them. To any policyholder who witnessed it or anyone who read about it, State Farm's response imprinted on them forever the message: State Farm *is* there.

It is not its slickness, polish, uniqueness, or cleverness that makes a brand a brand. It is its truth. By delivering its message in deliberately understated ads so unslick you are inclined to believe they must be true, and then living out the extraordinary promise of its otherwise ordinary message, State Farm has built an exceptional brand around a promise that people believe in for a very good reason: State Farm *lives* it.

Live your brand.

The Brand Placebo Effect

The man sees the tantalizing ad in the *Chicago Tribune*. "Grow hair!"

Noticing the trend of his hairline is backward, he responds by leaving his office early one afternoon to go to a clinic just off Michigan Avenue. He is triaged into an examination room, where eventually a young woman in a white coat enters. The man learns she is administering Rogaine free to men, as part of a "market test."

Would the man try the Rogaine for three weeks, she asks, and report the results?

The man happily agrees. He hurries home, opens the Rogaine, rubs it into his too-expansive scalp, and begins to wait. Three weeks later, he wakes up, walks into the bathroom, looks in the mirror, and feels a rush: New Hair! This stuff really works!

Or so he thinks.

The sobering fact is that our poor fellow's head is actually three weeks balder. Not one new hair has surfaced, and several hundred have disappeared, never to return. The nurse did not hand our confused man Rogaine at all; she handed him a bottle with a mixture of water, artificial coloring, scent, and lanolin.* This man was one of the controls in an experiment demonstrating the placebo effect. Tell people that a drug will make them feel better, then hand them a sugar pill with no curative properties in it at all, and a miracle occurs: A significant number will tell you that "the drug" did just what it promised.

What does this have to do with marketing? A great deal—indeed, it provides a critical lesson in perceptions and brands. This example suggests that one of the outcomes of successfully promoting a product or service is what we can legitimately call the Brand Placebo Effect.

We use a brand service. At the end, we feel happy with the service, comforted by our feeling that it accomplished just what we thought it would. But the Brand Placebo Effect tells us that our belief that something *will* do such-and-such leads us to believe that it actually *did*—even when it didn't.

Brands, then, are not simply tools for attracting business, which is the conventional view of them.

*In these tests, many of them performed on Merck's male baldness drug Propecia, 40 percent of men said the product that turned out to be the placebo slowed down their hair loss. One in three said it stimulated the growth of new hair. Those who used the actual drug, by contrast, reported only somewhat better results, 60 percent.

A brand does not merely attract clients, it convinces clients that they got just what the brand promised—*even when they didn't.*

Build a brand. Services are sold on faith, and brands create faith.

The Birth of One-Asset Companies

Consider this question: Are you more than your brand?

Treated as a matter of strict logic, the question may seem preposterous: You and your company are flesh and blood, years of unique learning, and perhaps some processes that make you more efficient.

But at the pure level of building and sustaining a business, what really are you?

Consider the John Hancock insurance company, founded in 1862 in Boston. Today, nothing about the original John Hancock remains; the original building is gone, and everyone who worked with the company before 1953 has left. Like every company, John Hancock can simply be viewed as an empty shell, through which people come and go. As one ad agency executive once said, "All our corporate assets leave the building every night."

What is that shell? It is the brand: the reputation of the company for integrity and performance, and other key characteristics. All around you, you now see this very fact carried to its logical extreme—of which the Sara Lee company is a perfect example.

Today, Sara Lee does not bake cakes. In fact, Sara Lee makes and manufactures absolutely nothing; it is what experts call "the assetless company." Sara Lee outsources virtually all its work. So what does Sara Lee do, and what assets does it own?

Sara Lee manages the Sara Lee brand—by far the largest, most valuable asset it owns. (It essentially leases its other great asset, its employees.)

Your service brand works in two directions: It works in the way we typically think, as attracting buyers with the brand's implicit promise of quality. But the brand also works at the level of the second key pool of prospects: prospective employees. Because you are more than your brand; you are the people who represent it, manage it, and carry out its promises, and the more compelling your brand, the more easily you can recruit that exceptional talent you need to continue to deliver exceptional results.

And so even if you view your business as nothing more than the people who go in and out the door every day, your brand is your most valuable asset.

Your business is your brand.

Labrador Retrievers versus Customers

Labrador retrievers, old friends, and most spouses are loyal. That about covers it.

Several recent articles suggest that some prominent American companies are suffering from a loss in brand loyalty. But by any acceptable definition of the word, loyalty rarely exists when applied to brands.

There is brand *habit*. When you go to the grocery store and virtually without thinking buy the same toothpaste, razor blades, and chocolate chip cookies, you are displaying brand habit. You appear to be an utterly devoted customer of Crest, Gillette, and Keebler, but in reality, you are scarcely thinking about your purchases at all.

There is brand *affinity*. Oregonians, even those relocated to distant states, show a marked affinity for Nike shoes, because Nike is headquartered in Oregon and Oregonians are clannish. Harley owners feel a profound affinity with what Harley Davidson represents, and a powerful desire to be thought of as a Harley driver. But because even most familiar brands have very little meaning, most people who consistently choose these brands feel no affinity with them.

Finally, there is brand *preference*. The family that routinely pulls into Burger King when it wants a quick, affordable meal displays brand preference. Mom and Dad feel no strong loyalty to Burger King; if a faster, better, and cheaper fast-food restaurant pops up, they'll start popping in there.

The task of even a small business, in light of this, is to focus on two things.

First, you need to perform with such a high level of consistency that people begin to feel a baseline confidence and comfort. They come to think of you not necessarily as a great thing, but as a fairly sure one. When you achieve that, you can achieve both brand habit and preference—both of which are desirable, but neither of which should be mistaken for loyalty.

Second, recognize that the meaning of your brand can attract people to you and increase their sense of linkage to you. Your brand can have meaning, however, only if you focus on what you want that brand to represent, and consistently present that to the world. If you try to represent yourself as all things to all prospects, your brand will have no meaning at all—and you never will be able to capitalize on anything at all.

Forget brand loyalty—but build a brand.

The Physics of a Brand

At the end of the tunnel they could see solid brick.

To virtually every observer, it appeared as if Apple Computer was racing headlong toward its death in the late '90s. The company's internal bickering, its decision not to license its operating system, and the omnipotent Microsoft had bitten into Apple. In 1996, the company managed to lose a stunning $1 billion. A year later, it sold only 1.8 million Macintoshes—less than half the unit sales of just two years before. *Business Week, Fortune,* and other leading business publications eulogized Apple in early obituaries.

But in 1998, those editors felt like U.S. congressman Bob Stump, who in June of that year had taken the floor of the House to lament Bob

Hope's death. Unbeknownst to the congressman, Mr. Hope was at that very moment eating his breakfast.

If you listened carefully, you could hear two sounds. Above the ricochet sound of Apple hitting bottom and bouncing back up, you could have heard the whoosh of marketing-textbook editors stampeding to their keyboards. They were racing to amend their chapters on branding before some observant second-year student raised her hand and said, "Professor, the book says that you cannot revive a dying brand. What about Apple?"

What about Apple? Apple's story suggests that like most rules, the dying-brand rule is stated too broadly, and thus misleads us. You almost certainly cannot revive a dying *weak* brand. No one has managed to revive moribund product brands like Schlitz and Pabst Blue Ribbon, or service brands like Braniff Airlines and Drexel Burnham Lambert. But these brands suffered a significant weakness in one of the three critical qualities of a successful brand: direction, breadth, and depth. The examples just cited illustrate the idea of direction: All were heading down. Consumers tend to jump on bandwagons heading up, and leap off those heading down. A brand with a positive direction attracts buyers; one with a negative direction repels them.

The brand's second critical quality is breadth, or familiarity. Coca-Cola is the world's broadest product brand; McDonald's and the U.S. Army are the two broadest service brands. Particularly in services, where the item being purchased is invisible and therefore difficult to assess before buying, the breadth of a brand is an enormous asset. It implies the service's widespread acceptance and continuous satisfactory performance over time.

Apple's story, however, illustrates the extraordinary influence of the third critical quality, *depth*. En route to Microsoft headquarters one evening, a researcher attempted to highlight the meaning of depth and the unique depth of the Apple brand by inquiring of fellow airplane passengers, "What do you think of when you think of Microsoft?"

Almost everyone answered the question with the same three free associations: "Big; rich fellow (Bill Gates); techies." These consistent definitions illustrate the little-commented-on weakness in Microsoft's marketing arsenal. Its brand has no better than a neutral meaning; it has no depth.

In contrast, the typical answers given to "What do you think of when you think of Apple?" were "Creative, fun, user-friendly, pretty cool." Apple's brand has exceptional depth; it's a meaning that others aspire to, traits that many people want to be identified with. Apple lacks the breadth of Microsoft, but clearly has shown more depth.

This depth of the Apple brand—its rich meaning to many prospects and owners—buffered the company's downward spiral. Saddled with an inherently weak brand like Braniff, Apple almost certainly would have declined faster. But the resonant depth of its brand and the remarkable loyalty that it inspired in its customers helped keep the company alive while Steve Jobs and friends in Cupertino fought to refocus the company.

In developing a brand, ask: What do we want our brand to represent? What attractive and desirable qualities should it embody? (A brand usually can accommodate not more than three meanings. Perhaps the world's deepest brand, Harley Davidson, has just two meanings, "male" and "rebel"— but what extraordinarily vivid and influential meanings they are!) Then imbue your brand with that meaning in everything your company does, from the sign over the door to the service and support.

Give your brand depth.

The Name Game

The name leaped from the ad in *Red Herring*, the technology business magazine.

I had never seen the name before—and never forgot it. Soon, the name seemed to appear everywhere—even though it didn't.

The name was Red Pepper, just two words among hundreds of words in a mergers-and-acquisitions ad. The ad was filled with financial tombstone rectangles, each tombstone referring to a merger or sale. One tombstone—just two inches wide and two inches high—simply listed People-Soft's merger with Red Pepper. Just one tiny mention.

Yet dozens of people like me never forgot that name: Red Pepper.

At the office of a Silicon Valley venture capital firm a few months later, I heard a quiet voice call my name. It was the voice of Monte Zweben, then an entrepreneur-in-residence at the firm, and before that, the founder of Red Pepper. Admiring his skills at nomenclature, I had to ask:

"What was that name worth?"

"More than we could ever have guessed," Monte said. "The effect was amazing. The name absolutely sparked interest in who we were and what we were doing. Whatever we were doing, people decided we were worth looking at."

Monte founded Red Pepper in 1993. On September 7, 1997, he merged it with PeopleSoft and learned what was in a name: in less than four years, *millions*.

But before we stop, it is worth probing further. What makes the name Red Pepper so effective?

Be distinctive in naming your business, too.

Out-of-towners who head to the nearest Burger King instead of the Convention Grill in Minneapolis or the Carnival in Portland—the great local burger places—behave just like the voters who choose the most familiar name on the ballot. Candidates win on name recognition; companies win on brand recognition. Both cases perfectly illustrate the Familiarity Effect—our tendency to choose what is most familiar to us.

How does a company become familiar to us?

You find the answer in our brain: Some names just stick there. Why?

In some cases, they have been drilled in. Pound a name into someone's brain often enough and the brain finally surrenders. Major advertisers spend over $100 million annually apiece just pounding the name in. We go to the store, see that very familiar name, and buy it.

But what if you are a marketer without $100 million just sitting around?

You choose a name that is "unique, sensory, creative, and outstanding," in the words of the authors of *The Brain Book*, an intelligent examination of how our brains work.

Red Pepper meets *The Brain Book*'s first test of memorability. While not utterly unique—red peppers obviously exist in abundance on produce shelves, after all—the name is a very unusual name for a company.

Red Pepper, however, meets another requirement for exceptional memorability. It is *sensory*. It engages four of the five senses. Red Pepper appeals to your sense of sight, taste, smell, even your sense of hearing—you can almost hear that crunch. Because the name triggered so many of the senses, it imprinted quickly on people's brains. In some cases, just that tiny mention in that huge ad did the trick.

Look for a name that people can see, smell, taste, feel, or hear—or better yet, all four. Be a Red Pepper.

WHY YOU ARE NOT OPIUM OR FROOT LOOPS

Many service founders strike out in search of the perfect name.

They fail because they try too hard.

They try for the name that captures everything about them—particularly their superiority—and that resonates with the creativity and surprise of names like Fahrenheit, Apple, Creative KidStuff, or Go.edu.

They end up frustrated because they start out wrong. Yes, they should explore the jungles for exotic or offbeat names; their search will assure them they have covered all the territory, and may inspire them. But these explorers must also remember that service names, like services, are not products.

The typical product possesses one signal trait: it is tangible. As a result, we buy products for their inherent qualities and their symbolic ones: the man who buys a Coach briefcase, a Cross pen, or a Hermès tie buys it partly because of how it performs, and partly because of what the product says about the owner. Many people wear product brands, and the savvy manufacturer makes sure that others see them. A Mercedes designer makes sure its symbols are in place so the car clearly announces "I am a Mercedes."

Services, by contrast, are invisible to everyone. We do not try to keep up with the Joneses' choice of broker, orthodontist, family therapist, or Internet service provider, because we have no idea who they chose. We use services almost by stealth. (Indeed, our relationships with therapists, doctors, lawyers, and priests are protected from public scrutiny by laws and rules of evidence.) Who knows—or cares, for that matter—which accountant does your taxes, which lawyer drafts your will, which dry cleaner presses your slacks, or which mutual fund companies manage your 401(k)? With few exceptions, we do not wear services like badges of status or means of self-expression.

Services differ from products in another way that influences their naming: *control*. You own the product that you buy. You control it. Your services, however, are more apt to control you. The doctor or dentist determines what you need, and when and how you receive it. If you seek advice from a service, you find yourself at the adviser's mercy. How do you argue, for example, that the statute of limitations does not apply to your proposed legal claim?

We crave control, but feel a lack of it with services, so we feel less comfortable in our relationships with services. We need their reassurance that they will use their control intelligently, and in our best interests. With few exceptions—our choice of amusement parks, comedy clubs, and some restaurants, for example—we need to know the service is serious, experienced, consistent, and reliable.

We now come to the final, and perhaps the most important, distinction between services and products: the aspect of *play*. Granted, we use some products as tools: a Subaru station wagon or a Craftsman hammer, for example. But we buy many more as *toys*. We choose even some of our most practical tools—computers, cars, and clothes, to name three clear examples—for the fun the manufacturers have engineered or branded into them.

How else do you explain the iMac, the computer that comes in five fruit flavors including tangerine and grape?

But rarely do we choose services playfully or frivolously. We are not looking for a moment's fun from lawn services, motels, airlines, financial advisers, or remodeling contractors. Fun sounds like a waste of our time and money. With some products, frivolousness is not only welcome but the driving force: consider Pet Rocks, Dilbert squeeze dolls, and Green Bay Packer cheeseheads. There are no Dilberts, Pet Rocks and cheeseheads among services, except those that entertain at children's birthday parties—and people take even that purchase seriously.

As a result, it rarely is wise to choose a playful and frivolous name for a service. (A service that violated this rule, not surprisingly, is a famous one that sells toys: Toys-R-Us.)

Prospects regard most services as serious business. A service must appear serious. Names like Red Pepper, Opium, or Purple Moon work perfectly for products with fun attached to them. Names like those will usually not work for a service.

Take naming your service as seriously as your prospects take the service itself.*

Few marketing tasks befuddle marketers more than naming their company or services.

The great temptation is to christen your company with a heroic and important name, like Pinnacle or Superior, or International Computer Solutions for a start-up based in Austin, Texas. These names reflect the erroneous belief that people buy how skilled you are rather than how much you can help them. Names like these are company-indulgent rather than customer-friendly.

*Yahoo! by choosing an almost frivolous name, seems to violate the general "no frivolous names" rule. Yahoo!, however, recognized that it was providing fun, which made its controversial choice appropriate.

Even worse, scan the bankruptcy notices in your daily paper. Do you notice all the superior-sounding names? You do—and customers instinctively associate hyperbolic names with second-rate companies.

Look for a name that makes the prospect, not you, sound important.

ORDINARY NAME, ORDINARY COMPANY

From the mouths of babes often come marketing gems.

Consider the following well-known psychological experiment. The researcher shows a baby several pictures. If the researcher keeps changing the pictures, the baby keeps looking. But if the researcher pulls out the same picture several times, the baby stops looking.

The baby almost certainly is demonstrating the habit that helps explain how our species has survived. Imagine a morning during the Pleistocene period. The first beam of morning sun warms Neanderthal Man's eyes and awakens him. He rises, drapes on his fur, and stumbles to the cave opening to determine if the weather will be good for hunting. He gazes east toward the sun just peeking over the mountain. His eye detects something due south. He turns quickly toward this something.

Fortunately, the shape is an asteroid that struck last night. "*That* was that thump," our caveman thinks, and continues to survey the landscape.

Why did the caveman turn so quickly? Because he detected something new in his environment. If our ancestors had not been acutely sensitive to their environment, they would not have survived to become our ancestors. Some of the new things would have eaten them. We respond to new things because we must.

The more commonplace you sound, the less interest you will attract. A familiar name, for example: 27 companies called Pinnacle are listed in the Minneapolis Yellow Pages. You also can find 46 Summits (this in a state without mountains by the way), 52 Alpha-somethings, 76 Pro-somethings, and 126 companies called Professional.

Do these companies get our attention? Do we remember them? If we do notice and remember them, we probably confuse them with other companies with similar names.

Appeal to the baby and the caveman. Say something new.

Sounds Like Trouble

Full Crumb.
Ree Lie Uhh Star.
Fay Shull Ass Thet Icks.

You wisely assume no one would ever give a company the names above.

But they did.

Those names are Fulcrum, the name of several products and services nationwide; ReliaStar, the insurance company; and Facial Aesthetics, the former name of a well-regarded Denver-based clinic providing minor cosmetic procedures.

Spell these names phonetically and you realize why you should never use them. The words each have at least one syllable that conveys a strong negative connotation. Aesthetics, thanks to the syllables *ass* and *ick*, ironically, manages to be one of the English language's least aesthetic words.

Similarly, you might call your bakery the Croissant Shop if you opened it in Paris. *Kwa Sahn* sounds attractive, sophisticated, and appetizing. In Boston or Portland, however, you become known as the Cross Ant shop—far less appealing and appetizing.

Before you name a service, product, or company, say your proposed name out loud. What do the syllables convey? What associations are buried inside the words?

This exercise will help you assess the feelings that the name might evoke—and clearly, those feelings must be positive.

Say your name out loud, and listen very carefully.

CHOOSE A NAME, NOT A PARAGRAPH

Ardent race car fans can assure you the following is not a joke.

Thousands of people attend a car race whose name might have been inspired by the Jan and Dean race car song "The Anaheim, Azusa and Cucamonga Sewing Circle, Book Review and Timing Association."

The race is called, seriously, the A-AI AC Delco Jani Express Cleaning Service 500.

Close your eyes for five seconds, then open them.

Now read the next line.

Repeat the name of that race.

At best, you remembered only the familiar name that already was stored in your memory (AC Delco) and the final word (500), because people best remember familiar names and the most recent events in their lives.

No matter how often you hear that name, you will not remember it. The brain cannot process it.

The race's organizers may have devised the most comical name in American marketing, and the most extreme example of names that are virtually unbrandable, because you cannot brand them in the place where branding occurs: the human mind.

For years, Pacific Applied Psychology Associates labored under this problem. Who could remember what they were called? In the late 1990s, a branding mentality took root in Berkeley; executives changed the name to Pathmakers.

Even its many thrilled clients could not remember the name of Applications Consultants Incorporated of Denver. Then the firm, which specializes in technology consulting to schools, changed its name to Go.edu—a name few people forget.

Now, prospects notice and process "Pathmakers" and "Go.edu" every time the names appear in newspapers, magazines, letterheads, and signs. Prospects are becoming more familiar with the names faster, and feel comfortable with the companies. Soon, these prospects decide that these companies are experienced and skilled. The prospects are listening more carefully, calling for the company's literature, and mentioning them to peers.

The companies grow. The name helps.

Keep your name short—eleven letters or four syllables maximum.

WHAT'S TOO MUCH IN A NAME?

Les Miz.
FedEx.
AmEx.
Phantom.
Deloitte.
Do you see the pattern?

These are the de facto names of services whose full names had more than eleven letters or more than four syllables, or both.

What happened? The human mind abhors longer names—and refuses to use them.

This is why Federated Investors in 1999 changed its name to Federated, Federal Express surrendered and shortened its official name to what everyone called it anyway, and why companies ranging from Personal Defensive Measures in Fredericksburg, Virginia, to Applied Medical Resources in Laguna Hills, California, are changing their names. The names do not work.

One of the few known marketing jokes is on the subject of brands that are too long.

Two leather-skinned Texans find themselves side by side in a Houston bar. They begin to talk and learn they both own cattle ranches.

"So what's the name of your ranch?" the first rancher asks.

"The Circle K," the second says. "What about yours?"

"Mine's the Lazy L Bar T Circle Q Sleepy C Triangle D."

"Jeez, you must have a ton of cattle!" the second says. "About how many head do you have?"

The first winced. "To tell you the truth, not that many.

"Most of 'em don't survive the branding."

To become a brand, keep your brand name short.

Brands and Performance

The bottom line: Do brands pay?

The University of North Carolina's business school recently studied the correlation between service practices and results—specifically, margins, cash flow, and return on assets. They found, not surprisingly, that the top service performers also generated the best measurable results.

The study, however, also suggested something else.

Hotels outperformed every other industry; their margins, cash flow, and return on investment, in fact, were markedly superior to those of every other industry. Experts on branding would also contend that hotels historically have been better at branding. Most of their executives understand brands and have invested heavily in developing and differentiating theirs. (Only fast-food restaurants, in fact, can match hotels for their emphasis on branding—and fast-food restaurants were not covered by the study.)

Media, industrial services, and retailers, which lagged behind hotels in branding, also lagged significantly in financial performance. But the three industries that performed the worst also proved to be the three that brand the least: health care, local government, and professional services. Indeed, in professional services it is rare to hear the word *brand* mentioned, even among those who are charged with developing new business.

Consider some recent service success stories: Kinko's, Starbucks, Yahoo!, Regis hair salons. In each case, branding was a critical part—in the case of Yahoo!, *the* critical part—of the business strategy. In each case, the brands have created powerful franchises through which the company can distribute additional services and products. In each case, the brands have created powerful barriers to entry for aspiring competitors.

Granted, to survive, each company will also have to deliver good service at an acceptable price. But in each case, the brand has helped ensure that the company will survive—and profit far more than companies and even entire industries that ignore the illogical but overwhelming influence of brands.

You ignore the power of branding at your peril—and your expense.

THE FALLACY OF QUALITY

Here is a short list of the computers that had far more power and storage than IBM's top-of-the-line computers:

In the 1980s, both the Victor 900 and the Hewlett Packard HP 150 had more power, storage, and memory than the IBM did. The DEC (later Digital, now Compaq) 100 had more power and storage. Today, Victor is gone and DEC/Digital has virtually disappeared into its merger with Compaq. Hewlett Packard continues to thrive, but as a printer and peripherals company rather than a computer manufacturer.

The best, in short, lost. Quality lost. Clear feature superiority lost. Better mousetraps lost.

So what won?

Two things. First, IBM was known for its service—for the sheer speed and competence with which it would fix whatever was broken. And so IBM came to be known as the safe choice, immortalized in the now-famous ad slogan, "No one ever got fired for choosing IBM."

That line clearly reflects IBM's second major weapon: its brand. IBM PCs became known not for their quality and superiority, but for the simple fact they were IBM. You bought IBM PCs not because of what you thought about them—chances are you knew only enough to make you dangerous. You bought the computers because of the brand behind them. You didn't buy the computers; you bought the brand.

Brands trump quality.

TODAY'S BEST BATTLE
OF THE BRANDS

No wonder those Californians shout "Yahoo!"

If you could turn so few resources and so few people into so huge a company as Yahoo!, you would scream "Yahoo!" until your neighbors called the police.

What does Yahoo!'s rocketlike ascent reveal? Just what you needed to hear, but never expected.

To understand, conduct this test.

Ask twenty Internet users "Which search engine do you usually use first?" This is what you will probably hear:

Fifteen will answer Yahoo!

Two will say Excite.

Three will mention one of many other search engines.

No one is likely to mention Northern Light or Dogpile. Perhaps one person will have heard of either service.

Probably no one will say AltaVista, the preferred choice of the nation's most expert searchers: America's corporate librarians.

If you believe that better services ultimately win, your results seem stunning.

If you perform simple side-by-side searches using identical search words, you will discover that despite its popularity and shocking wealth ($38 billion in market value at this writing), Yahoo! does not equal the other four engines for speed, breadth, accuracy, and "cleanliness." Excite and AltaVista are faster and cleaner; Dogpile and Northern Light uncover more good sources.

So much for better mousetraps.

Yahoo!'s competitors opted for quality—for superior performance. Yahoo! opted for brand and scale. In fact, Yahoo! executives admit they have pursued an almost pure brand strategy, as three telling anecdotes suggest.

If you work for Yahoo!, for example, and need to paint your car, the company will pay for the paint job—if "Yahoo!" is painted somewhere on it.

In 1998, a top Yahoo! executive hired landscaping contractors to plow her existing garden under and plant a brand-new one, with only purple and yellow flowers—Yahoo! colors.

And then there's sheer cheek. Perhaps to promote the company at the gym, a top Yahoo! executive had the Yahoo! logo tatooed onto an unusual site: his buttocks.

For years, Yahoo! lost millions, much of it simply getting its name out. It published *Yahoo!* magazine and ensured that bookstores and newsstands displayed it—effectively creating Yahoo! billboards. The company ran millions of dollars of television commercials each year that delivered a simple, brand-driven message: "Do You Yahoo!?"

And we do.

We Yahoo! not because Yahoo! is a superior product, but because it is the superior brand. It promotes itself so relentlessly that when you think of searching, you think Yahoo! And Yahoo! makes searching sound fun—an amazing accomplishment, given the sheer unfunness of waiting for downloads and enduring freezes, collapses, and other glitches.

THE THIRD KEY:
PACKAGING

The Blue Fox Revisited

Let's return a third and final time to the Blue Fox (from page 77), and that marvelous freeze-dried coffee.

The evidence suggests one reason that diner loved the coffee was because the meal cost so much, and the restaurant had such an exalted reputation, she assumed the coffee had to be delicious. And so it tasted delicious to her—even though it wasn't.

Another influence was working on the guest, however—an influence that occurs every day in your business. She entered the restaurant and was taken with the ambience: the fine bone china, the linen tablecloths, the elegant trio playing a splendid arrangement of a Brandenburg Concerto, the razor-sharp edges of the waiter's white-on-white tux shirt.

To borrow from that old song, the eyeball's connected to the taste buds. You see quality, and then you taste it—even though the quality is utterly missing. Appearances do not merely attract us; they transform our experience. We think tall men are wiser, and elevate them to positions of power in companies. We associate every possible virtue with physical beauty; millions of people are certain O.J. Simpson is innocent, because he looks like a movie star.

This section explores this remarkable power of packaging, and our susceptibility to visual cues and clues.

Oranges and Greens

You know that lab coats and stethoscopes make doctors better practitioners.

You realize that the artificial color on its peel enhances the flavor of the orange inside.

You have learned that handsome hairdressers are more skilled than homely ones.

Of course, you are now insisting, "No! I don't agree with any of that!"

It's natural to think that you never judge books by their covers, oranges by their peels, or doctors by their lab coats. Perhaps you are one of those rare, self-actualized individuals who consistently sees through surfaces and into the essence beneath.

Perhaps. But even if perceptions never distort your view of reality, when you are marketing you must act as if others are not as wise. Because they're not.

For example, I'm not.

I fly to New York City. That night, I will tell an audience at the Learning Annex that people's preference for the oranger of two oranges shows that packaging works in irrational ways.

As John McPhee relates in his book *Oranges*, oranges are picked when they are green and then sprayed with chemicals to transform their green color to a vivid and appetizing orange. The vivid orange of an orange peel is, in short, a packaging trick.

I know this. I had read McPhee's book. I know better than to choose the oranger orange.

So what happens? I arrive in midtown Manhattan on the day of the speech. New to speaking, I decide I need props. I come across a produce vendor selling fruit from a sidewalk cart. Perfect! Oranges! They'll help me make my point about packaging.

Being frugal, I know I'll eat my props after the speech. Unable to reach the oranges at the back of the vendor's cart, I ask the vendor to pick out three oranges for me.

The vendor grabs an orange brighter than a Syracuse football helmet. He places it in the brown paper bag, then grabs a paler-looking orange. I nearly leap across the cart to seize his arm.

"No, no, not that one! *That* one," I say, pointing to an orange the color of a Ventana Canyon sunset.

Then I catch myself. I'm en route to a lecture in

135

which I will tell an audience that the color of an orange does not matter. "A yellow orange is just as juicy," I will say. "You cannot judge a book by its cover."

And yet *I'm* judging a book by its cover. I *know* I should not; I *know* better; I *know* color makes no difference.

But what we know often does not matter. *We act on prejudices and habits, not on knowledge.*

Ask a serious golfer "Which course in America would you most love to play?" Your odds are good he will say Augusta National in Georgia.

Every golfer yearns for Augusta for its signature trait: its velvety, greener-than-green fairways. More than any other influence, in fact, Augusta National explains why golf courses in Omaha and Olympia look greener by the decade.

Country club members have pressured their greenskeepers to pour the members' billions into their fairways, hoping to duplicate the Augusta Effect. The best grass is the greenest, the thinking goes. To help the world know that its members are rich and important, country clubs are quickly turning their golf courses Augusta green.

Greenskeepers and horticulturists understand the irony here. Grass works like human skin: the darker you try to make it, the more you threaten its health. You make grass greener by watering it constantly and strafing it with chemicals. Constantly watered grass never has to dig down deep to quench its thirst; the water is within easy reach. So that grass does not need to develop the long roots that make it stronger. The shallow roots also create root-free spaces just below the surface where insects and pests can set up camp, and later attack the grass. These attacks fire the first shots in the unending war between the pests and the greenskeepers, which the attackers often win in very dramatic form, forcing the closing of courses for entire years so the fairways can be reseeded, overwatered, and killed again. In Great Britain, where Augusta Envy is replaced by St. Andrew's Envy—a lust for fairways the color and topography of the moon—and where most of the watering is performed by North Sea clouds, these disasters rarely occur.

Will American golfers ever learn? Will prospective country club members learn to look beyond the apparent beauty of a course and see the real healthiness of lighter-colored grass and the sensibility of the greenskeepers who keep it that way?

Not likely. However fragile and superficial beauty may seem, beauty has muscle. It seizes us; we cannot get away. We insist we can see beyond the surfaces.

We can't.

Your prospects can't either.

We act under the spell of packaging.

You practice and study. You spend years learning more and becoming more skilled. You think that if you and your company just get better and better, the world will see it and reward you for your talent. And then they look at your coat and your shoes and your teeth, and draw their conclusions—even when they, like me in search of oranges, know better.

Your packaging is a set of cues and clues from which people draw conclusions—often, seemingly ridiculous and totally unjustified conclusions.

What clues are you sending?

Are you sure?

Look as great as you are.

Beauty Trumps Quality

Just a car? Perhaps. But the Jaguar XKE tells us who you are and what you buy. The XKE, yards long and seemingly only inches high, has captivated people since it first stunned the guests at the 1961 Geneva Motor Show.

You can appreciate the car's artistry even more if you tip it until its famous snout faces straight up. Seen this way, the car's shape—its almost liquid finish and distinctive orbs and curves—clearly resembles the works of the great twentieth-century sculptor Brancusi. Car imitates art.

Ironically—but perfectly for this discussion—the XKE's other claim is to infamy. Any car buff knows some variation on the old joke "You do not actually own an XKE. Your mechanic does."

The XKE represents another victory of packaging over quality. At a minimum, if function really mattered, you'd buy a car to get you there. An XKE often got you nowhere. Millions have bought them, however; many more still covet them.

We crave beauty.

Tiny children choose pretty colors to paint with. They stare at pretty women, but not at homely ones. Beauty wields so much power that it inspired Nancy Etcoff, a psychologist on the faculty of Harvard Medical School, to write *The Survival of the Prettiest: The Science of Beauty*, which makes this compelling case that we have a genetic predisposition to judge books by their covers, cars by their silhouettes, and people's character by their faces.

We are born craving beauty.

And yet how often does this subject arise in most businesses? We have quality initiatives, but do we initiate continuous *beauty* improvement programs? Do we accept our prospects' prejudices—their often subconscious belief that the more beautiful alternative is better?

Or do we defiantly insist that if we just build better mousetraps, the world will buy them?

Build prettier mousetraps.

THE PURIST'S PREJUDICE

"It should not matter!" the purists insist. Logically, who can disagree?

These purists include the attorney who argues that only her skills should matter to clients, the engineer who lobbies for function over form, and the Bauhaus-inspired architect who deplores anything designed only to please the eye.

"Substance and excellence are all that should matter," the purists insist. They treat style, design, and form as excessive and often manipulative: visual hocus-pocus.

The purists miss the point, however, by misstating it. Beauty is not simply form without function.

Ask yourself: Between a skyline of concrete and glass boxes and a skyline like Chicago's, would you ever choose the ugly alternative? You would not, because Chicago's is far more beautiful, and beauty performs a powerful function: It pleases us. It makes us happier.

A grape iMac performs like a beige box—and yet it does more. It makes us smile. It makes us feel a little better. It makes our lives better, for reasons beyond reason.

A consultancy's Class A monthly rent may end up increasing its clients' fees 8 percent. Those clients are paying for advice; they should not have to pay for the cherry paneling and the just-cut red tulips in every office. But clients do not merely appreciate the tulips. The tulips—which seem to be mere form, lacking in substance—enhance the clients' experience. Their cheerful color and fragrance make the clients *feel better*.

In serving your clients, consider this:

Can you do anything more important than that?

To make your service better, make it more beautiful.

The Number One Mistake

Business executives often ask marketers, "What one change would help most?"

For smaller businesses particularly, but larger businesses often, the answer is: Look like you want to succeed.

A 1981 ad for Omnibus interiors created by the Borders, Perrin & Norrander agency captures this opportunity perfectly. Over a photo of a dilapidated office door that read "Attorn y" in cheap press-on Helvetica letters, the "e" apparently long gone, appeared this memorable reminder about packaging: "The longer your office says struggling young attorney, the longer the struggle."

Eight years later, an ambitious real estate agent asked another advertising agency to make him rich. He announced he wanted to attract this flood of business by spending only from cash flow. The agency executive deduced, from this prospect's chattiness on the phone and habit of three-hour lunches, that the prospect's cash flowed only in trickles.

The prospect clung to his penny-wise strategy. He marketed a little here, a little there. Ten years later, his business perfectly reflects his marketing strategy: a little here and there. Fame and fortune are as distant today as they were then. They may be beyond reach.

A third peek into the weakness of timid marketing can be seen at the Monday morning meeting of elite venture capitalists. Premier venture capitalists behave like the management of the Carolina Panthers football team: they get a franchise, build a colossal stadium, hire several high-priced free agents, and try to win it all—in their first year. (The Silicon Valley pursues this strategy so relentlessly it has earned a shorthand, GBF—Get Bigger

Fast.) Outsiders, particularly people like that real estate agent, scoff at such strategies.

Why do venture capitalists follow them?

Because they want to succeed.

And they do. You can search decades before you find a business more financially rewarding than venture capital.

Where do service businesses err? They spend timid—and end up looking timid.

To understand the perils of timid marketing, think about how most people invest. When we have money to invest, where do we invest it? In companies we believe in. Conservative investors choose companies that will be around. Aggressive investors invest even more in companies they have confidence in. They believe those companies will thrive.

We invest in companies we believe in. And we know that others do the same.

What impression do you make, then, when you appear to have invested very little in your own business—in your brochure, offices, business cards, presentations, advertisements? You're saying you lack confidence in your own enterprise. You are not confident enough to invest in yourself.

What happens? If you—the person who knows more about your company than any prospect could—lack confidence in your business, why should your prospects put any faith in it?

They shouldn't.
And they don't.
If you believe in your business, show it.

The Small Stuff

How do we decide who people really are—and whether we should retain their services?

We look for clues.

When a writer profiles a celebrity, for example, and wants to tell us who this celebrity really is, he observes and reports details. What shoes is she wearing? Is she wearing eye makeup? Does she serve water in simple Crate and Barrel glasses, or in Waterford crystal?

What's on her mantel: her Oscar, or pictures of her teenage children?

Does she bite her fingernails?

We try to hide ourselves behind large and obvious things: our house, cars, and other outward gestures. Knowing this, when we want to discover the real person behind the veil we look for the tiny details.

Consider, as one vivid example, the heel.

What could be more obscure than a heel? The cartoon character Linus once hinted at the heel's obscurity—and his own attempts at cultivating his image—when Lucy one day asked him why he shined only the front of his shoes.

"I care what people think of me when I *enter* a room," Linus answered. "Who cares what they think when I *leave*?"

Linus was wrong. People noticed the back of Linus's shoes well before he left. In fact, for decades it was precisely to a man's heels that people looked to determine his station in life. People knew that a man might continue to wear an expensive gold pocket watch and rich-looking silk tie for years, but that he would skimp on replacing the heels of his shoes when cash was short, thinking no one would notice.

But people did more than notice. *People learned to look for that very detail.* Thus entered into English the expressions "well-heeled" and "down at the heel." People looked at people's heels—a tiny detail—to tell who they were.

The next time you visit a Nordstrom store, sit in one of the chairs and ask, What's different about this chair? The company ordered it custom-built, at great expense, with a firm seat slightly lower to the ground than a standard chair's. Nordstrom designed these chairs after noticing how much effort it took customers to lift themselves out of heavily stuffed chairs.

Why did Nordstrom spend hundreds of thousands of dollars to custom-make its chairs? Because they understand that tiny details attract and keep customers.

"God is in the details," Mies van der Rohe is famous for saying.

Business is, too.

Copy your prospects: Watch your visible details.

The Shock of the Not-New

It's shocking, really.

We know a picture can speak a thousand words. We probably know of the countless studies that show people remember images far better than they remember words.

So why do most service firms choose cheap, generic, and meaningless images?

Why do the majority of American health care services use the same image in their brochures?

You know the image: an apple-cheeked, almost wrinkle-free, salt-and-pepper-haired couple, frolicking on golf-course-green grass, all but shouting "Who needs Viagra? We're with Sam's Health Plan!"

What additional 992 words do these images convey?

That Sam's Health Plan hires the same fifty-five-year-old models—the ones who turned prematurely gray—that all the other health care companies hired?

That Sam's Health Plan actually helps people stay healthy? (Now, *there* is a strong claim.)

That Sam's Health Plan found the same stock photo catalogs that most other health care companies use?

Faced with the opportunity to convey three pages' worth of solid information, what do these firms—and firms in hundreds of other industries—say? Virtually nothing. Typically, they convey the exact same virtually nothing that their competitors convey. No one expresses some point of difference, some selling point, some piece of evidence that at least suggests "We are different from our competitors. Take a look at us."

At a minimum, try to say at least several hundred words with your pictures.

Choose images that at least imply that you are different.

And at a minimum, choose images that convey quality.

Images speak volumes—but only if you let them.

Scale and Intimacy

Walk the Main Street of Disneyland. Ever noticed the trick being played?

Disney knows that the first task of pleasing a client is to make him comfortable. So they have designed the buildings to make you feel that way.

At first, they seem like amazing duplicates of what you assume buildings on old Main Street looked like. Like everything else in the park, the buildings are freshly painted and spotless. You are not even thinking about their most distinctive feature, however: They are not duplicates. They actually are two-thirds scale; they appear to be typical buildings, but they are smaller—deliberately.

The Disney architects knew that people feel most comfortable in intimate surroundings. The sheer size and scale of New York City, for example, makes many first-time visitors wish they had booked earlier return flights home. Disney made the buildings small to make visitors feel bigger, more important, more in control.

You can feel this same force at work in many of the leading "extreme value" retailers in smaller towns. Resisting the conventional wisdom of value retailing, which looks for economies of large scale and large selections, these retailers operate in almost comically small spaces. The average Dollar General or Family Dollar store occupies just 6,500 square feet. Dollar Tree pushes the number even smaller, to an average of just 3,900 square feet—smaller than thousands of American homes. If you ask some random customers why they shop there, they might say value. But those values are available at other stores. Probe a bit further, and you will get the more important answer:

"I just feel that I belong here."

The size feels right; it feels intimate; the person feels bigger and more important there. And so you legitimately say they do not go to these stores for the merchandise; they go for the feeling—the feeling of comfort, of belonging, of being significant.

You can create that feeling with space, with design, with attitude. But however you create it, you will reap rich rewards if you create an entire experience that makes the client feel important.

Create the environment that will create in your clients the crucial feeling: their feeling of importance.

Is It the Ball Game, or the Ballpark?

The critical service in running a baseball team seems obvious: hire good players, play winning baseball, and the fans will beat a path to your turnstiles.

Baseball is the product; forget the packaging. Just have them play in a simple concrete stadium with Neo-Soviet architecture: the old Seattle Kingdome and the Minneapolis Metrodome immediately come to mind as good, awful examples.

The old Seattle Mariners and the current Minnesota Twins, clinging to the view that their service is providing winning baseball to watch, can try to blame their players for their poor attendance. But they can do this only by ignoring Baltimore.

Through brilliant insight or sheer luck, the owners of the Baltimore Orioles reached the seemingly preposterous conclusion that what surrounded the baseball field was almost as important as the players playing on it. In 1989, the construction began on what became Oriole Park at Camden Yards—a triumph of architecture so complete that the *New Yorker* magazine devoted four pages to it shortly before it opened in 1992.

But what may be most significant is not just the revolutionary design, which managed to make a beautiful new park look eighty years old, but the people who started filling it from Opening Day. Since Camden Yards opened, an Orioles fan from out of town has felt little hope of getting even a high-altitude seat in right field. Attendance the first year was 3,567,819—the highest in the major leagues, despite the park's location in a city one-eighth the size of New York.

And the performance of the team? Not so hot. The Orioles won 89 games and lost 73 the first year in their new home. The next year, they won 4 fewer games.

And attracted 77,000 more fans.

The Orioles sold their service like no other team in baseball. They did it not by offering a winning team, but by offering a remarkable package and a wonderful visual experience—right down to the logo of the 1890 Orioles handsomely burnished into each aisle seat.

By focusing on their prospective buyers' eyes, and creating a visual experience, the Orioles proved that baseball is more than a game—just as accounting, law, and medicine are more than just professional services.

Ask yourself: How is your ballpark?

What does what you offer look like?

151

Does it look like excellence? Does it fit the prospect's image of an extraordinary service?

Does your package, your place, and even your person enhance the experience?

Your package is your service.

THE FOURTH KEY:
RELATIONSHIPS

A Laura Nyro Encore

Let's return to the Laura Nyro concert at Stanford University in 1970, which illustrates the overwhelming power of this fourth influence on people's perceptions.

We should have loved her concert. Every key element—price, brand, and package—was in place. The $4 ticket price, peanuts by today's standards, was caviar for two college students strapped with huge tuition bills. The singer owned a brand name and had written brand-name songs. And the packaging was perfect; Stanford's handsome Memorial Auditorium.

The curtain opened—and quickly, all expectations were dashed. We left unhappy; the music had sounded *bad*, somehow.

What had failed?

The relationship had—Nyro's with us. She refused to try to connect with us. She wouldn't address us, thank us, look at us. She seemed untrusting, even though she was only terribly shy. She established no feeling of community. She seemed so unsure, we even questioned how skilled she really was. We felt more uncomfortable than she appeared.

The elements of a great relationship were missing: affinity, trust, apparent expertise, magic words, passion.

This chapter will show that while price, brand and packaging may trump quality, there is one force in services even more overpowering: relationship.

Business Is Personal

For years, we flounder around with the faith that a unique body of knowledge called "business" will lead us to prosperity.

This makes us weak prey for charts, graphs, matrixes, and maps that imply we might find a mathematical formula for success, with A+B=$ being the ideal.

If only it were so. If only business operated like math or organic chemistry, we could figure it out sooner. Mathematics and organic chemistry abound with well-established principles, rules, theorems; you can figure much of both out with relative ease.

We know acid will turn blue litmus paper into red. We know that lengthening one side of a right triangle will have a predictable effect on the length of the hypotenuse. Business, on the other hand, is based on people—something about which we know very little. We are left to traffic in hunches, hopes, and best guesses. We play the percentages and diversify our marketing portfolios, to increase our chances that our big successes will offset any small failures.

Business is about people. A service succeeds when it makes significant numbers of people feel their lives are somehow better than they would have been without that service. The role of marketing is to ask, How might we do that? How might we make people feel better? What is it that they want, and need, and how might we answer that?

In meeting that need, we succeed not just in making money, but in experiencing the great satisfaction that comes in serving someone other than yourself.

Business is about people.

Caring versus Conquering

Seventy years ago, many people even in developed countries were short of food, clothing, and shelter. After the Depression ended, those people owned most of those things, and began seeking luxuries. Life accelerated. And something even more significant to the modern marketer occurred: Life spread out.

The advent of technology that allowed us to go anywhere, fast, led people to go everywhere. Once, in our not-so-distant agrarian past, entire families lived their whole lives on one plot of land. The trip into town was an event; the trip to a distant city a rarity.

All that has changed. Today the typical American family is scattered across the country. And the consequence of this radical disruption of human ties is this: What people most miss today in their lives is connection.

No focus group or survey will tell you this. No one will tell you they would like to feel more connected with you; the desire is too personal, the request too strange. Yet survey people about a wealth management service. Ask them to rank the firm's return on investment among their criteria for choosing a service. You will find that investment performance ranks about sixth—three places below "the firm representative's apparent desire to develop a long-term relationship with me as a client."

Survey clients of a law firm. Ask them to rank all the reasons they continue to work with the firm. "Fees" typically ranks several notches below "promptly returns my phone calls." The lawyer who returns the phone calls communicates that the client matters—that the relationship is important. To the client, that connection matters more than the fees—as controversial as law firm fees are.

To make and keep a sale, make and keep a powerful connection.

THE IMPORTANCE OF IMPORTANCE

Pacing in the center of a beautiful new classroom at the University of Chicago's business school, the speaker punctuates his remarks to the employees of Allegiance Health Care with references to their competitors McFaul & Lyons and CSC, and observations about the hidden fears of COOs, operating room supervisors, and directors of nursing who are their prospects and clients. The employees listen intently—and leave very satisfied.

By making those specific references to Allegiance's business, the speaker has not demonstrated more skill, more wit, or even provided more useful information than the other speakers. The employees—the clients for the speaker on this day—have responded well for more personal reasons: because the speaker, by taking the time to study their company and industry, has made those people feel *important.*

Don Lothrop, a successful partner with the Menlo Park, California–based venture capital firm Delphi Ventures, may owe some of his success to a productive Monday morning habit. Each Monday, he calls the CEOs of the companies he has invested in. He often has no particular agenda, except to remind them that he is there to help. And every Monday, Don's clients are reminded of something even more critical: they are *important* to Don.

Several of the country's premier men's clothing salespersons, employees of Barney's in New York, enclose a thoughtful note with each package they send their customers. Now and then— not so often it appears contrived, but often enough that it feels meaningful—they send brief notes thanking them for their business. They make their clients feel *important.*

Assuming that the health care speaker, the venture capitalist, and the men's clothing salesman all meet their clients' basic needs—for advice and for shirts—these clients will value those services deeply, not because the professionals have satisfied their basic needs, but because they have satisfied a more personal and more emotional need: the need to feel important.

Make your clients feel important.

Your Favorite Drink

Asked to explain the appeal of country clubs, the founder of Club Corporation International revealed the appeal of many services, including cheaper ones.

"It's a haven of refuge," Robert Dedman told Diana Henriques of the *New York Times*, striking the first strong chord. Huge numbers of great services recognize that most people today find that much of life is too fast, hard, and indifferent. These marketers create oases.

The Oasis Strategy may be most obvious at Disney World. In designing Disney World, Walt Disney recognized that his original theme park, Disneyland, was slightly flawed. Walt was certain that his parks should be refuges from the world. Disneyland, unfortunately, soon found itself surrounded by cheap motels and heavy traffic—acres of concrete and noise. Sobered by the experience, the Disney team decided that they had to create a true oasis in Orlando.

And so they began, parcel by parcel and under cover of fictitious names, purchasing far more land in Orlando than the Magic Kingdom and other Disney attractions would ever require. You cannot miss the results of this effort today. As you circle the property seeking your hotel, you find yourself driving through vast acres of undeveloped land. Once inside your hotel, you walk to the window of your fourth-floor room, look out, and see nothing but this island. No Orlando, no strip malls, no freeways—nothing to impede your sense that you are secluded in a refuge from the outside world.

In discussing the emotional allure of Club, Dedman went on to highlight an even more salient point that marketers can translate into effective action. "A club should be a place where the staff addresses you by name at least four times during your visit," he said, "and always remembers your favorite cocktail."

The casual reader might race by Dedman's last line as a throwaway. Dedman did not intend it that way. He was serious—and right. The staff at the perfect club *does* remember your favorite cocktail. That gesture distinguishes the perfect experience from an ordinary and less satisfying one.

That bartender gives you something valuable: the sense you are important. You matter enough that he remembers your favorite drink.

The world grows bigger every day, so we grow smaller. We feel lost in the din. As that world grows bigger every day, our desire to feel important grows into a need. The client who feels important feels loyal.

Create an oasis.

The Curse of the Bad Client

Perhaps you still think the only bad client is a deadbeat.

In most service businesses, the real costs of a bad client never appear on the books; some are partly hidden and some are time-released, waiting to spring on the unsuspecting accounting department at any time.

Let's look at the real and sometimes nearly catastrophic costs of the bad client.

The obvious first cost is psychic. Working with the client is a toxic experience: it is physically and emotionally draining. It makes those employees involved with him distracted, unproductive, and unhappy.

The next cost often is overlooked. It's the cost that occurs when that client is passed on to another group of employees, often under the pretext that they have the unusual skills to deal with this special client. What it really means is these employees are lower in the pecking order—and have just been reminded of it. They have been handed the peacetime equivalent of latrine duty. Their morale suffers. In many cases, they are also angry, envious, or downright hostile toward the fellow employees who just off-loaded the problem client.

Morale suffers more.

This move, while it may temporarily keep the first group of employees from fleeing the company, intensifies the problem. The client is now dealing with a new set of faces who are less familiar with his problems and needs, and clearly more junior than the previous team. The bad client grows worse, with all the problems that creates internally.

In the meantime, no one is calculating the dollars lost because of all the time lost in meetings over dealing with the client, meetings demanding changes, meetings with the client to address his grievances, meetings to decide what to do, meetings trying to coax the new team into working with the ogre, and meetings upon more meetings, none of them truly productive, and all of them at the expense of real work for good clients.

As segmented as a company's organizational chart may appear, morale never observes these tight boundaries. Morale has the qualities of an airborne virus—it leapfrogs walls and cubicles and moves through the ductwork. And while you cannot estimate the real cost of low morale, you can know its salient trait: its real cost far exceeds its apparent cost.

Now, the virus escapes the building—another huge and underestimated cost. The bad client voices his displeasure to others: friends, colleagues, fellow employees, members of his professional associations, the executives in his weekly foursome, and many others.

This word of mouth spreads further, invisible to the service provider. The balance between good and bad word of mouth now tips strongly in the direction of bad. People who might have been prospects write the company off their short list, and subtly influence others to do the same.

Meanwhile, attending to the bad client diverts the company from two key tasks: serving its loyal and valuable clients, and performing the tasks that can produce more clients. These are opportunities lost, a loss no service provider accurately measures. That's one major reason why balance-sheet accounting fails to clearly reveal how a service is really doing.

Ultimately, of course, the client leaves. Accounting often takes another unexpected hit when that client's receivable, which the company had been treating as income, goes unpaid. A dispute, ranging from almost polite to downright hostile and litigious, follows.

The company loses more. Even if it recovers from that client, the client essentially takes that money back—and many dollars more—by dissing the company to anyone who will listen.

Bad gets worse. The employees feel angry with management for continuing that relationship and handing them latrine duty. Job satisfaction drops. The experience drives several valuable and well-trained employees closer to leaving for another company; its grass looks greener.

You must spot the bad client *before* he becomes a client. If you are accepting every client who strolls in the door or calls on your phone, you are sowing the seeds of your own destruction. If you are allowing them to linger in your halls, you are multiplying their cost to you—daily.

Refuse bad business—and get rid of it fast.

WHY TOM PETERS WENT MAD

Even casual Tom Peters fans have noticed his radical metamorphosis. Peters began in *In Search of Excellence* as a gentle teacher who explained; he proceeded in subsequent books to serve as an adviser, then as an exhorter, and finally he became an evangelist, shouting at the top of his lungs.

This is what happened. Everyone said, "We agree with you, Tom." Then they went out and ignored him. Nothing changed; even the excellent companies declined.

Tom has witnessed what we've all witnessed, if we've taken a look around. Here are just a few of the utterly bewildering marketing blunders I have seen in the last six months:

The title slide for the key presentation to a major client misspells the client's name. (Honest.)

Purported brand extensions make no mention of the brand name.

A company invents a name that no one can pronounce.

A company adopts a logo that looks fairly appealing on a fifteen-foot banner but is illegible when used in a quarter-page newspaper ad—a medium the company plans to use within the next two years.

A twelve-page brochure never explains exactly what the company does or how it might be different from its competitors.

A Fortune 500 company illustrates its multimedia presentation to a Fortune 500 prospect using the very same cartoonist and cheap clip art that a local grocery store in Minneapolis uses in the flyers it sends out.

An advertisement lists sixteen reasons we should buy a particular service, positioning the service as both the premium and the most affordable service, as well as the best—without ever explaining what "best" might mean.

A stockbroker from a famous brokerage pitches Coca-Cola as "a terrific value at this price." But he cannot say what Coke's current price/earnings ratio is—the most common tool for measuring a stock's value.

A company president insists that each client should be treated as very important. The next day he sends his clients a holiday card with no note, only his signature.

And so, as Kurt Vonnegut once said, it goes.

Marketing mistakes are so prevalent that it can honestly be said that principles of marketing are honored more today in their breach than in their observance. Dozens of executives praised *Selling the Invisible* by saying it preached what they had been practicing for years. But then you visit their companies and learn that, while rules are certainly made to be broken, these companies have gone overboard—breaking rules in every category, from positioning to naming and branding, all the way through to client service.

And in breaking the rules and ignoring all his advice, they have driven Tom Peters mad.

What's happening? The Lake Wobegon Effect, a well-recognized and almost universal psychological affliction: the tendency of most people, particularly men, to overestimate themselves. Most men think they are much better than average-looking, just as most executives and marketers think they are performing much better than their competitors.

But then you visit their company and read their marketing materials. You realize that their service is not positioned. Its distinctions are buried. The company fails to reveal its key evidence until page three. The company name meets few of the criteria used to judge a name. The brochures read like rough drafts.

All this, and the potted palms in the lobby are dying and the receptionist—perhaps frustrated by the difficulty of today's crossword puzzle—is surly.

It's events like these, I suspect, that drove Tom Peters mad.

Several companies—Morningstar, Putnam, Marriott, McDonald's—consistently demonstrate they "get" marketing. They demonstrate it by earning spectacular returns on their marketing investments. But these exceptions are just that: exceptions. The rest of us, it has to be said, kid ourselves.

We are victims of the Lake Wobegon Effect.

And it is costing us billions.

Get much, much better.

The Eight Keys to Lasting Relationships

1. NATURAL AFFINITY

Seek out yourself.

Interview the rainmakers in an accounting, law, or other professional service firm. Ask them to list their most loyal clients and enthusiastic referral sources. Then ask the rainmaker to describe each person. Two interesting patterns usually emerge.

You spot the first pattern among the clients. *They sound remarkably similar to each other.* In one interview, a rainmaker described each of his six most loyal clients with only minor variations on this theme: "Slightly liberal, graduate degree, devoted parent, avid reader, somewhat introverted but cordial, pretty sophisticated tastes, mildly perfectionist, not particularly money-driven or -oriented."

All six clients fit that profile. Even more significant, however, is the fact that a seventh person fit the client profile: *the rainmaker himself.*

In the corridors of business, you occasionally stumble across that rare bird, the consummate salesperson. Ross Perot is one. Richard A. Eisner's accounting and consulting firm in New York employs another. Both men possess that chameleon-like quality that allows them to instantly adapt to people, find their common ground—and assure the prospect that they both stand solidly on it.

That person, or the firm that can rely solely on that rare bird—or chameleon, actually—can ignore this section. Everyone else can benefit from realizing that people just like you will do more to build your business than any other clients will.

(In hiring, however, do not choose your clones. It deprives your business of "hybrid vigor," the hardiness produced in a species by the mating of different types—what might be viewed as the flip side of the perils of inbreeding. Hiring people just like you amplifies not only your strengths, but your weaknesses as well.)

Choose the clients who are most like you.

Avoid Blind Dates

If you would never select a particular service yourself from the Yellow Pages, never take a client who responds to you from the Yellow Pages. Clients generated purely from advertising, and particularly from Yellow Pages advertising, are the least loyal clients. They are the most apt to leave early, often before they become profitable, and you end up serving them at the expense of good clients.

A Yellow Pages reader has no affinity with you. She has simply happened upon you. The odds of success are minuscule, your chances of longevity not much better.

Avoid blind dates.

Avoid the Fickle

Clients who have run through several similar service businesses before choosing yours are probably impossible to satisfy. Historic business wisdom reminds you not to hire someone who has switched companies often.* Conventional social wisdom urges you to avoid as a spouse someone who has been divorced many times. Why apply different thinking to a prospective client? If you interview the client and ask who they worked with last, and their response unsettles you even a little, know this:

Working with them will make you even more uneasy.

To gain loyal clients, find loyal people.

---

*The explosion of high tech, the proliferation of lucrative stock options, and a near zero percent unemployment rate seems to have changed this rule, at least temporarily.

The Failing Relationship, and What to Do About It

A consultant salesperson from a Fortune 500 company, feeling troubled, raises her hand with a question.

"I have this client," she says—and no one listening can miss the negative connotation of the word *this* as she begins her question. "Things started out okay, but they seem to have gone bad, and I really don't know what to do about it. What do you do about a relationship that is going bad?"

She has answered the question with her introduction. The relationship is going bad because she does not really like this person. The speaker probes.

"If you could have only twenty clients, is this person one you would choose?"

"Well . . ."

"Now, be honest."

"Well, I mean in a perfect world, I guess not, but the world isn't perfect."

"Do you like this person?"

"Yes."

"No, I mean, do you really *like* this person?"

"Well, no."

"So what you are asking me is, 'How come this person I don't like doesn't like me?' Isn't this a lit-

173

tle like coming to me as your marriage counselor, and you tell me 'I don't like him,' and your husband said, 'I don't like her, either,' and then you asking me what's wrong?"

This woman is trying to separate business from the rest of life. Like most of us, she assumes that business responds to a different set of rules: the set that says work is hard, work isn't supposed to be like play, and that business relationships are different from personal ones.

But as I told her, we all tend to like those who like us. Novelist Wallace Stegner once captured this with wonderful subtlety when he wrote "I liked him. (He liked me.)" Stegner was reminding us that we like those who like us, and do not like those who do not. This questioner's relationship probably could never be saved; unlike people in a bad marriage, people in a bad business relationship have little incentive to stick it out. Her company needed to reassign someone else to the business, or just let it go.

Counseling can work for couples; businesses, however, don't have the time.

Seek clients you would want as friends.

Embracing the Inevitable

From 1992 to 1997, our agency converted 91 percent of its serious inquirers into clients.

This achievement sounds like great business.

It wasn't.

This batting average certainly suggests a knack for turning prospects into clients. What it conceals, however, is a violation of what amounts to a law of nature.

Whatever term you may use for it, "chemistry" in human relationships—and a service business is basically a collection of human relationships—ultimately governs our behavior and dictates which relationships endure and which do not. Some people have an unusual capacity for a significant number of successful relationships; some have little capacity at all. But in every case, the percentage is limited—and *not* 91 percent.

Our percentage suggests we were terrific salespersons. Less obviously, it suggests we refused to evaluate. We accepted and converted almost every serious inquiry. Not surprisingly, the chemistry sometimes blew up. We failed to recognize the importance of affinity.

In the spring of 1998, one such client ended her association with us. The project had gone well: we had provided good advice and insight into several of her immediate problems. But we realized from the start we were too different. The problem was not that she was unpleasant, dishonest, or difficult; in fact, she was charming, smart, successful, generous, and open-minded. But an inexplicable something, some difference, kept us from completely understanding each other.

She did us an enormous favor. One day, we will spot each other in an airport, renew our acquaintance, and at least tacitly recognize the simple fact we learned that spring: *Everyone isn't for everyone.*

Accept that no one is for everyone, and find the best fits.

Enough About You—Let's Talk About Me

A longtime employee of one of the world's most famous service companies recently revealed her view of her company's history, and its influence on the company.

"I have a slogan for us," she confides. "A hundred and twenty-five years of tradition unmarred by progress."

Her company is proud of its long history, with good reason. What it should be sensitive to—as should every other service in the world—is that longevity alone doesn't mean much.

As a prospect in 2000, do you find it relevant that

the company you are dealing with was meeting customers' needs during the Grant administration?

A similarly meaningless message is the anniversary message. One of the world's premier technology service companies recently marked its twentieth year in business. Rather than spend $500,000 telling the world that it was the preferred vendor to 25 of America's 100 largest corporations, it instead told the world—few of whom had ever heard of the company—that it, like the two-person consultancy down the street that is one late receivable away from bankruptcy, has been around for twenty years. (Sports fans, take note: The Chicago Cubs haven't won a World Series in ninety-two years. And based on their performance, one can only conclude they have grown worse from experience rather than better.)

As a prospect, I do not care about how special you think you are. I care about what you can do for me, and how much you might care for me. Your years of history, your commitment to excellence, your president's message to shareholders, your various statements of commitment or mission—about these, each of your prospects feels just as Tommy Lee Jones felt in *The Fugitive* about Harrison Ford's shouted insistence that he did not kill his wife.

"I don't care!"

Do not communicate for the sake of communicating. Do not tell us something about your company because you have heard other companies making similar proclamations. (The majority of these companies are only doing it because some other companies have done it, or because they have an advertising budget and need to say something, and have no idea what else to say.)

Tell me something I really care about.

Tell me about me.

Faux Relationships

Imagine receiving the following letter. Assume the information about you is accurate. Monitor your feelings as you read it.

Dear Mr. Jones:

Because you drive and love the new Lotus 540 and are an avid reader of travel magazines, we want to alert you to a wonderful new publication: *Lotus Lover* . . . We know both you and your wife, Susan, will appreciate its timely articles, including lifestyle features on topics of great interest to you, such as German beers, Cuban cigars, and golf in your native state of California.

How do you feel?

Invaded. Someone has purloined information

about you. Like most Americans, you are fanatical about your privacy and dislike outsiders peeping into your life. You hate that people are recording your buying habits, because they reflect other habits of yours that are none of their business. The letter makes you fear that businesses are tracking your more personal habits and purchases, too.

How else do you feel?

Anxious. A huge corporation is pretending to know you. You feel about the authors of this letter the way you do about people who become too familiar too soon. You recognize that healthy people observe boundaries; this letter has crossed one.

These letters can be created through the magic of databases, the cleverness of freelance writers, and the tactics of "relationship marketing." Like too much of marketing at its worst, this very term defrauds the public. The only "relationship" this letter suggests is a bad one. The author knows nothing of the person with whom he is "developing this relationship," any more than I understand and like someone who I happen to know reads *Time* magazine, enjoys Sandra Bullock films, and avoids red meat.

The wordsmiths behind "relationship marketing" have corrupted the word *relationship*. It is genuine relationships that we must develop with customers and clients.

A feigned relationship is worse than no relationship at all.

Go slowly. Relationships take time.

2. TRUST

Trust is the key to any successful relationship. We all know that.

But what is trust?

We know it is a feeling: the feeling that we can depend on another person. But what produces that?

Predictability

Any close acquaintance of a dysfunctional person at least intuitively recognizes the first element: It isn't the dysfunctional person's worst behavior that damages the relationship, it is the utter inconsistency—and therefore, *unpredictability*—of the behavior that's the problem. You cannot depend on the person to be one thing or another; he will surprise you, and ultimately make you so wary that you pull away.

In successful relationships, each party can predict the other's behavior, even the bad behavior. The husband of a woman who suffers heavily from premenstrual syndrome typically adapts; he knows that at a particular time each month, she will resemble Linda Blair in *The Exorcist*. He can predict it, even depend on it. The relationship survives. The partner of the alcoholic, by contrast, can predict nothing; the worst can happen anytime.

Successful services tend to be predictable, and several spectacular successes have built their empires on that trait. McDonald's provides the obvious example. You may not absolutely love the McNuggets and the supersize shake, but you know that no matter where you order them, the nuggets and shake will always taste exactly the same. You trust McDonald's; McDonald's is utterly *predictable.*

To build trust, build consistency—in everything you do.

Integrity

We say we value integrity, and many people do.

We value integrity among our social peers because at least subconsciously, we realize it has a heroic quality; it often requires courage, after all, which is not always easy for us to summon.

But in business, we value it for different reasons.

When we are prospects or clients, we prize integrity because a service that keeps its promises makes at least part of our lives more predictable. We know that our favorite cleaners will have that black sport coat tomorrow, for example, so we can plan on wearing it the following day.

We do not have to worry about the coat, or about having something appropriate and clean to wear that day. We can check that item off our list. We can worry about one less thing.

A service's integrity, in short, makes our lives more convenient, more comfortable, more predictable.

Write down every pledge you make to a client—and be sure that you keep it.

Protectiveness

You learned the third trait of a trustworthy person from painful experience.

You divulged a secret to someone you trusted. And you learned you shouldn't have.

A person can act consistently and with integrity and yet still fail to earn your trust because she was not protective.

You fully trust only those people you know will protect you.

This is why lawyers, doctors, psychotherapists, priests, and some other professionals have lobbied for, and earned, privileged status in courts of law. If you confide in one of these professionals, he does not need to reveal what you said to him—even if that confidence involves a capital crime that you committed. In fact, it is a breach of his professional code of ethics.

This very trait defines professional services: They are ethically and legally bound to preserve any secret a client reveals to them. These services are protective—by law.

The law may not obligate you to protect your particular clients and preserve their confidence, but if you're a great service, you do it. The most obvious breach of this obligation occurs every day, often unbeknownst to the offending service. A man and woman from John Doe Company make a sales call. During that meeting, their prospect mentions a Bill Smith at ABC Incorporated. The man and woman proceed to regale the prospect with stories about their experiences working with Smith and ABC. The typical prospect laughs along with them. The salespeople leave confidently, knowing that a good belly laugh is always a strong positive sign.

But the prospect chooses a competitor. His laugh, it turns out, was half-nervous. What made him anxious was the fear that *he* could be the next Bill Smith—the next victim of that company's failure to keep not only confidences confidential, but also the details—good and bad—of their relationship.

We place our trust and confidence in services that protect us, for the reason suggested by the parallels in the words *confide, confidential,* and *confidence.* Our greatest form of confidence, after all, is our belief that a person we confide in will keep that matter confidential.

In great client relationships, the client knows that you will act predictably, act and speak with integrity, and do nothing to harm her—ever. A great service, then, is protective. It regards its clients not simply as gold, but as glass; incredibly valuable but frighteningly fragile.

Assume that everything a client tells you is between the two of you. And if the relationship ends, make sure that your obligation to be discreet continues.

Loose lips sink enterprises.

3. SPEED

The story of the flying computer has implications for all of us.

Sitting in his home office at ten o'clock one night, the executive feels a sudden urge: He wants a new computer. Like most computer users, the executive does not want the new computer eventually, or even pretty soon. He wants the computer—of course!—right now.

He grabs his portable phone and a recent MacWarehouse catalog. He calls the 800 number prominently displayed on almost every page.

"I'd like the new Performa," he says.

The MacWarehouse representative confirms the item, the price, the executive's American Express card number, and other details. In less than five minutes, the deal is closed.

At eleven the next morning, an Airborne Express deliveryman knocks on the executive's front door. He is holding a box containing the new Apple computer.

The event changes the executive's perception of speed in this new age, and his expectation of all service providers. That change can be expressed in the thought balloon above that executive's head as he signs for the delivery.

"If I can get a seventy-pound, two-thousand-dollar computer overnight, from New Jersey to Minnesota," he wonders, "I should be able to get a double cappuccino in real time!"

The executive may sound only half-serious. But like so much humor, his remark hits our funny bone because it hits home. Why are some services so slow?

The faster things are done, the faster we expect them. The delivery of everything is heading toward real time—instantaneous delivery—because we expect it.

If we can get computers overnight, we should be able to get close estimates almost instantly. We should get proposals in two days. A copy of the new regulations on defined benefits plans in seconds.

In his 1970 book *Future Shock*, Alvin Toffler predicted an immediate future when life would be speed, and that future arrived so fast it proved Toffler right. Time is money; seconds are precious—particularly to the bulk of our population, that famous "pig in the python," who are in the last half of their lives and the first years of making each minute count for more.

Faced with this obsession with speed, the company that has been struggling to implement total quality programs is well advised, ironically enough, to slow down, then stop. Over the next six months, put aside your arduous efforts to define "quality," a huge challenge all by itself. Instead, look at every crucial process and every place you provide service and ask, "How long does it take to complete that?"

"How long must the client wait?"

Now ask, "How can we cut that in half?"

And when you accomplish that, ask, "How can we cut it in half again?"

In deciding what your customers really want,

and who they really are, you might look over their shoulder as they use the Internet.

You'd learn something very revealing.

They don't scroll. Few people ever hit the arrow to scroll down to actually read all or even most of the information that they retrieve. They tend to read only what immediately appears in the box. Then they move on to a new site.

These are fast times, everywhere. To answer the needs of your prospects and clients, you must get fast.

And then get faster.

WHAT *USA TODAY* KNOWS

You may deride it as McPaper—many critics do—but *USA Today* has one thing every business covets: satisfied clients.

USA Today gives millions of people what they want. In doing so, that paper reveals a lot about people—the people you are trying to reach.

They are busy.

Not long after landing in America 170 years ago, Alexis de Tocqueville asked: "What is an American, this new man?"

Observers appalled by what they say is the degradation of our culture—the "dumbing-down of America," as they often put it—should know that if de Tocqueville was right, things in America have not deteriorated; they have stayed the same. For the French politician and historian wrote: "Americans prefer books which can be easily procured and quickly read, and which require no learned researches to be understood."

Americans rush; we always have.

We are 200 million Sergeant Joe Fridays: We want "just the facts, ma'am," clearly and rapidly. We want to be engaged, and even amused—but quickly. This explains *USA Today*, almost a microwave version of a traditional paper, with stories that end where most stories in other papers begin.

Selling the Invisible and this book reflect a similar belief, and the best sales and marketing communications do, too: Tell me, in a way that stops me, engages me, quickly and clearly informs me—and moves on. Skip the balderdash, the puffing, the filler: *Tell me.*

Tell me the same way crime novelist Elmore Leonard (*Get Shorty*) writes books. Asked to explain why his books were so popular and so easy to read, Leonard answered:

"Simple. I just leave out the parts that readers skip."

Clients frequently ask how long their key sales brochure should be. The best answer is, "Use as many words as you need to say exactly what the readers want to know—*and not one word more.*"

Communicate like Elmore Leonard and *USA Today*. Catch my eye, catch my attention, and quickly tell me what I need to know.

Tell me—quickly and clearly.

Mach One Life

The tortoise's win was a fluke.

To fully appreciate the acceleration in our lives, pick up the wonderful book *Accidental Empires*, published in 1992. Robert X. Cringely's book intelligently describes the new computer technologies and the emperors behind them.

When you reach the end of this book, published such a short time ago, you may close the book, pause, then shake your head.

You realize that in those 200-plus pages, describing companies that have become household words as well as products you'd never heard of, Cringely left one tiny thing out.

He never mentioned the Internet.

Poor research? Hardly. Cringely never mentioned the Internet because very few people were even thinking about it in 1992, and no one had yet produced a viable consumer product or service.

Life today changes so rapidly that a technology that now dominates the business pages, front pages, and even variety pages, and surrounds us with World Wide Web addresses on commercials, billboards, and even in David Letterman and Jay Leno's jokes, was merely a glimmer in a few technophiles' eye just a few years ago.

You must constantly be alert to rapid change, and its imminence. Perfectionists particularly must adjust to this changing order, because sometimes, "perfect" means "pretty good but incredibly fast." A familiar expression in the Silicon Valley and among venture capitalists captures this shift:

"Fast is better than accurate."

4. APPARENT EXPERTISE

One warm April day in Dallas in 1997, a woman took her Siamese cat to her veterinarian for routine inoculations.

The vet noticed something the cat's adoring owner had missed: the cat seemed to be walking just slightly out of balance. Concerned, the vet began probing the animal with his fingertips, beginning at the spine. He slowly worked his fingertips up to the neck, and then from the neck to the ears. Then he stopped suddenly, and began to probe behind the cat's right ear.

The doctor became convinced that there was a

tiny growth behind that ear, a cyst that could be malignant. He explained this to the owner, then anesthetized the cat and opened an incision behind its ear. The vet located the growth, lanced and removed it, stitched up the incision, and later that day sent the cat home.

He had saved the cat's life.

As was the clinic's practice, the owner was given a survey. Among the questions was this simple one: "How do you rate your veterinarian's medical skills?" The owner had the typical 1-to-10 choices, with 1 being least competent and 10 being the most.

The doctor's fellow veterinarians would have scored him a 10. Most agreed that most very capable veterinarians would have missed that diagnosis, and the cat's tumor would have become fatally inoperable.

How did the client rate the vet? A 7—pretty good, but certainly not excellent, much less exceptional. How could this be? How could an expert doctor performing beyond reasonable expectations be perceived as a mere 7?

The answer was in his coat. He didn't wear a lab coat that day; he wore a Madras shirt. Pet owners give the lowest scores for medical skill to vets who fail to wear lab coats; the next lowest to those who wear blue lab coats; the second highest to those who wear white lab coats.

And which doctors are perceived as the most skilled and expert by pet owners?

The doctors who wear white lab coats *and* stethoscopes—by a wide margin.

You're only as expert as you appear.

The Power of Clarity

In our little hamlet of Neah-Kah-Nie, Oregon, my surgeon father built a legend.

This was the legend, as I often heard it from my friends: Dr. Harry Beckwith, Jr., was considered one of America's three best surgeons. (Every time I heard the story, by the way, the number was three.)

Worshipful of my dad, I believed the story. How could I think otherwise? Of course one of America's three greatest surgeons practiced in Wheeler, Oregon, population 287, two hours from the nearest teaching hospital, and with no other surgeons to learn from since he had arrived there fresh from his residency at Johns Hopkins.

How had Dad's legend grown?

The patients my father had treated had spun it. They had experienced him as a remarkably skillful doctor, and had started and spread the story. But what was it that they had experienced that had caused them to do that?

I can answer that question fairly objectively, and from experience. During my youth, I went to Dad to have splinters removed, a broken finger set, and my left foot stitched up. In my late twenties, I frequently sought his medical advice on my routine runner's ailments of stress fractures and tendinitis.

As I reflect on those conversations, my dad's gift comes vividly into view: He was a masterly teacher. Whenever I went to him with an ache or pain, he could perfectly explain, in nonmedical language, the hurt, the cause, and the treatment. He could make it vividly apparent why the ailment would require three weeks to heal, and why ice and elevation would speed the recovery.

After hearing a Dr. Beckwith explanation, a patient never had to say, "I'm not quite sure what you meant there." Dad's explanations of medicine were not medical gibberish; they were verbal gems of total clarity.

That gift begat the legend. People regarded Dr. Beckwith as an extraordinary doctor because he was an extraordinary explainer. Communicating clearly is the essence of creating the impression of competence, skill, and mastery. A service provider's ability to explain what he does, rather than to do what he does, is what most influences a prospect's impressions of his skill.

From Tillamook to Atlanta

That Tillamook County residents considered Dr. Harry Beckwith, Jr., one of the nation's most expert surgeons does not prove that prospects regard the clearest communicator as the most "expert" service provider, however.

For the added evidence, we turn, aptly enough, to the courtrooms, and to Dr. Richard Fuentes.

Dr. Fuentes serves as a principal in Decision-Quest, which specializes in jury consulting. For several years, DecisionQuest teams devoted thousands of hours to finding the answer to every trial lawyer's question: What is an expert?

More specifically, lawyers wanted to know what the "market" thought. What makes a juror think that one expert is more expert than the other—and therefore more apt to be believed in the typical battle of experts that often decides the outcome of a trial?

For years, lawyers have assumed the answer was credentials: an advanced degree from an exceptional university, bylines in the top professional publications, and the other evidence we naturally assume spells "expert" to us and everyone else.

We assumed wrong.

Thousands of jurors forced DecisionQuest to

accept the surprising but unavoidable conclusion: Credentials do not matter. (In fact, some impressive credentials have a negative influence on jurors.) What mattered? Who did people think was the more expert expert?

The person who most *clearly* communicated her expertise.

Granted, a few people are swayed by sesquipedalianism. The rest of the population, however, seems to live by a simple idea: If you're so smart, why can't you speak clearly?

Communication is not a skill. It is *the* skill. The best way to demonstrate your expertise is clearly.

Gary Larson captured it perfectly with a "Far Side" cartoon.

Larson was lampooning an owner who was talking to his big Irish setter, but he could easily have been describing all of us, talking to our prospects.

The owner says, "Bad dog, you bad bad dog, how could you do this!! You know you are not supposed to touch this, you ARE NOT a good DOG!"

A "thought bubble" emanates from the dog's head that tells the reader what the dog actually hears:

"Xmxmxmfrmdme **dog**, xmskksmxkskmx **dog**, mxmxmsmxkskmx mmxmms . . . xmxmmx **DOG**!"

Larson's Irish setter offers the perfect metaphor for Every Prospect, Year 2000. As marketing and salespeople, we assume that if we say it, it gets communicated. But we only communicate what the prospect understands. And today, prospects too often hear "Xmxmxmfrmdme dog, xm-skksmxkskmx dog!"

A classic and true example: A Merrill Lynch financial adviser stops by one night to advise a couple on a new investment. The wife is a former Big Six CPA and an MBA with a good grounding in investing and finance; the husband frequently advises many of America's top financial services and investment firms.

The adviser, in his well-rehearsed and carefully crafted presentation, lays out the advantages of a European sector, large cap mutual fund. Periodically, the adviser notices the husband or wife nodding knowingly. This series of nods and their firm and enthusiastic handshake as he leaves their home almost propel the adviser out the door with glee.

As he is congratulating himself on his sale, the couple are sitting at their dining room table. The husband turns to his CPA wife. "So, what did he say?"

"I don't know," she tells her financially astute husband. "I thought *you* knew."

"Beats me. I thought *you* knew."

Far too often when you walk out a prospect's

door and feel like clicking your heels, your prospect is saying just that:

"I have *no* idea what that was about."

Do they ever tell you they were confused? Of course not. That would be admitting they didn't understand a carefully rehearsed and deliberately stated presentation that you obviously have given hundreds of times to people who understood what you were selling, and bought it.

Who wants to look like the one fool in a hundred?

Not you. Not I. And not your prospects.

More than you know, your prospects don't get it. ***You must be clearer. Much, much clearer.***

Words

Name the famous service that uses the slogan, "Accomplish everything of which you are capable."

The service is the U.S. Army. That credo, translated into ad language, is "Be all you can be." Conservatively, those five words have been worth billions of dollars. What if the Army had chosen instead to exhort young men (and now women) to "accomplish everything of which you are capable"?

Nothing. Prospective recruits might have seen

197

the tanks and then heard the words at the commercial's end, but the words would not have penetrated beyond their ears, and few would have been moved to act.

"Be all you can be," on the other hand, passed through the ears en route to the heart and soul, where it lands like an anthem, a call not just to arms, but to achievement.

The ideas in these two slogans are identical. Yet the effects could not be further apart.

Especially when people cannot see what you are offering, words matter.

Craft, sand, and polish your words religiously.

The tendency of people to overestimate themselves—the Lake Wobegon Effect—shows up again when communication skills are involved.

Every advertising copywriter quickly learns that most people think they can write and speak well; they simply delegate that task. We assume our proficiency in English from the fact we have used it all our lives. If we cannot write or speak English well, our thinking goes, what *can* we write or speak?

Unfortunately, this is a very good question. Venture capitalists know the problem. They usually read only the first page of a typical business plan; that page says to them, "Read no further; we are either confused about our business or unable to describe it well."

Editors of legal publications know the problem. At an average law school, where the students are well above average in intelligence and language skills, the typical student paper submitted to the law review cannot be published without radical editing.

Prospects for information technology services know the problem. They can understand most of the brochures from companies in the information technology outsourcing field, but cannot find a clear answer to their most important question: What makes your service different?

Obscurity abounds. Ask a car dealer to explain a lease. Ask an investment adviser to explain the percentage and dollar impact of management fees and commissions on real return on investment. Ask a publisher how royalties on books purchased in Saudi Arabia work.

We are encouraged to express our feelings. Perhaps we should be. But we must be able to communicate clearly; to write and speak not just so we are understood, but so we cannot be misunderstood. And with few exceptions, schools fail to teach that.

Few people teach that, so few learn it. And yet the evidence is overwhelming, from the coast of Oregon to DecisionQuest's facilities in Georgia, that communicating clearly is your most indispensable asset. That ability will lead prospects and clients to conclude that you are just what they want: an expert.

Assume everyone in your company could communicate more clearly—and invest in learning how.

Communicating Your Special Expertise

A surprising lesson, learned the hard way.

Our doors opened in 1988 and we immediately acquired our first client, a national collection agency. For several months our work helped generate business for them. One April afternoon in the following year, however, the client's marketing director called with bad news. He was leaving the company and a new director would be replacing him—a danger signal to a service like ours.

Six months later, we received confirmation of the signal.

"We've chosen another agency," the new director said.

"Oh. Who?"

"We are a family business," he said. "Mater & Pater specializes in family businesses. They were hard to resist."

Being diplomatic, we did not let this client know that no marketing or advertising agency specializes in family businesses. Or that "knowing" family businesses in marketing is like "knowing" brunettes in shoes sales: useless. Unfortunately, "apparent" specialized knowledge mattered to that prospect—as it does to most.

The unique value of even worthless specialized knowledge can be explained by this fact: Every industry, like every person, believes itself—its markets, processes, challenges—to be unique. Businesses and people believe that previous experience with similar businesses and people helps, even when it doesn't.

The title "specialist"—however fraudulent, irrelevant, or even comical—packs a persuasive wallop. You cannot rationally justify, or argue with, the success of hair salons that specialize in blondes, benefits consultants who specialize in law firms, or ad agencies that "know" family businesses.

For this reason, most start-ups or small firms feel they must communicate a specialty. The specialist's implicit claim, "We do not know everything and do not try to, but we *really* know [blondes, law firms, family businesses, fill in the blank]," can win business against larger and better-qualified competitors. The prospect finds herself saying, "Well, that little firm is honest enough to admit it's not good at everything, but it is *great* at this."

This thinking, like so much human thinking,

isn't rational—as the collection-agency example clearly shows. But however irrational it is, understanding and capitalizing on this "specialist bias" can launch a small firm faster than any other single tool.

Find your specialty—no matter how narrow it is—and communicate it convincingly.

The Apparent Expertise of One Specialist

To determine what you might be considered a specialist in, inventory your key employees' background and knowledge.

In 1988, when I launched my solo business, my background inventory looked like this:

Oregonian
Son of surgeon/medical school professor and registered nurse
American history and humanities major, Stanford University
College journalist
Former personal-injury and medical-malpractice attorney
Former self-coached champion distance runner

My knowledge inventory, which is linked to my background, looked like this:

Law and legal practice

Medicine and medical evidence (from father and legal practice)

Physiology, exercise physiology, nutrition, and kinesiology (from self-coaching)

Journalism

Money and investing

Social sciences: psychology, sociology, and anthropology

American history

Given my background, it is not surprising that my first significant professional clients were law firms; that my largest group of initial clients were medical-product manufacturers; that among my most acclaimed efforts were three historical films.

It is equally unsurprising that as my business has evolved, my clients have been professional service firms and services directed at educated and affluent audiences (a Greek travel agency, *Utne Reader* magazine, a high-end jewelry store, a college scholarship foundation). And that more than 25 percent of my annual business has come from investment and financial firms.

A marketing firm tends to evolve to match its background and special knowledge. This happens by both intent and accident. We did not seek out medical-device companies, for example, or any of the high-end consumer services. We expressly targeted only law firms. We sought out some of our clients, but many of them found their way to us. The key to growth, as frequently mentioned in the business literature of today, is knowledge. What do you know? What do you know very well?

To identify your business opportunities, identify your background and knowledge, and which prospects would be particularly attracted to either or both. What would they assume you know from your background? (A Minnesota lawyer colleague of mine has been quite successful in marketing his services to North Dakota farmers by stressing that he grew up on a farm. He knows farming, the farmers decide, and they send him work.)

Before you make a sales call, take inventory. You have more in stock than you realize.

But you say, "I am not in a knowledge business." Let's say you sell electronic fencing for pet owners—what difference does your knowledge make? As it turns out, a great deal.

On its face, Invisible Fencing is a product. It's an electronic device embedded in the ground that surrounds a yard and keeps pets from racing into streets by giving them a shock when they approach the boundary. But like so many products, Invisible Fencing has actually become a service. Its prospects can choose from among several competitive "products," which they cannot easily tell apart. What prospects can distinguish, however, is the salesperson's knowledge of dogs, specific breeds of dogs, and the way each breed reacts to the fence and the training that comes with it.

In fact, the Invisible Fencing company primarily sells its skill at working with and training the dog to deal with the fencing. Wisely—like the ad agency that approaches a family-owned-business prospect by demonstrating that it really knows family-owned businesses—Invisible Fencing's field staff stress that they really know the unique traits of Labrador retrievers, Lhasa apsos, and Belgian Tervurens, and that they adjust their training accordingly.

Not surprisingly, the company invites leading dog experts and trainers to its annual meetings, to add even more to the field staff's knowledge of various breeds and how to train them.

When the discount hardware store sells a fence, it's selling the fence. When Invisible Fencing sells a fence, it's also selling the value of its knowledge of different dogs and the best way to train them so that the fencing will work—and so that the dog will stay home and safe.

Instead of thinking about value-added, think about knowledge-added. What knowledge can you add to your service, or communicate about your service, that will make you more attractive to prospects?

Identify *all* your knowledge, and add it to your service.

Get To It

Successful marketing communications vehicles such as brochures, ads, and presentations immediately tell a prospect exactly why he should do business with your company rather than with someone else's—or with no one at all. Delay, fumble, or mumble hollow claims or still hollower expressions of mission and philosophy, and your prospect will put the brochure down—and you with it.

In your key communications, you must immediately state your most compelling claim to expertise.

Then you must offer the concrete fact that most strongly supports it.

For useful reference, we call this the Key Claim and the Key Proof. Like the description of your company that passes the Elevator Test—the statement you can make between the first and eighth floors that clearly communicates what your company does—the Key Claim and Key Proof succinctly state the strongest reason someone should work with you and the proof that you can deliver on that promise.

Beginning in the fall of 1997, Pathmakers, Northern California's largest behavioral health company, prepared to expand. Clearly, they operated in one of the "softer" service areas. How, after all, do you prove that psychological consulting works? Fortunately, during its fifteen years in business Pathmakers had made a practice of surveying its patients. These surveys provided the proof: Their patients reported that they felt significantly better. Pathmakers' files also contained data on overall patient satisfaction with behavioral health services—and Pathmakers' patients were more satisfied than the norm. These happy events provided Pathmakers' Key Claim and Key Proof:

"Pathmakers helps people feel better, faster."

"In independent surveys, 91 percent of our patients say they are improved or very much improved—a level of satisfaction that substantially exceeds recognized industry norms."

This Key Claim and Proof became the centerpiece for all the company's marketing communications.

But in today's microwave/fax/hurry-up world, you must do more than simply make those statements. You must make them *immediately*. Hesitate or bury the claim in paragraph three, and the reader flees. The prospect insists on getting to it; she is conditioned to believe that salespeople who really have an offer will communicate it immediately.

Get to it. State your claim strongly, confidently, and immediately—or it might never get heard.

5. SACRIFICE

Roger's rush seemed nice, yet hardly momentous at the time.

Asked to deliver a summerweight sport jacket to a Minneapolis business executive, Dayton's salesperson Roger Azzam attempted to comply, but Dayton's tailor told him that despite the tailor's promise to have the jacket finished by exactly that minute—noon, October 22—the jacket was not ready.

Roger returned from the tailor's back room and broke the bad news to the executive. The executive looked crestfallen. (One wonders why. By October 22 in Minneapolis, Minnesota, no one will need a summerweight sport jacket for at least seven more months. But human beings want services when they are told to expect them, rather than merely when they need them.) Roger sensed his client's disappointment, spun around, and sped back to the tailor. In seconds, Roger was back.

"Your jacket . . . will be ready . . . in five minutes," Roger said over pauses to catch his breath.

How did Roger's customer feel? Satisfied? Delighted?

Neither word adequately conveys the customer's reaction. Roger had essentially paid the customer more than the customer was owed. After all, the intense Mr. Azzam, clearly in his fifties, seemed to have risked his life over a silly sport coat.

So how did the customer feel? *Obligated.* Roger had evoked the executive's sense of reciprocity—the feeling that if someone does for us more than we have earned, we must do something nice for him in return.

Which is just what the executive spent the next five minutes doing. He picked out a brown sport coat he did not truly need; and a tie, shirt, and slacks to go with it. Roger spent two minutes running back and forth to the tailor's room; to reciprocate, the executive gave Roger's employer $870—or $26,100 per hour of Roger's time.

Sacrifice is the cement of human relationships. Nothing bonds someone to you more.

Your Clients' Sacrifices

How much must you sacrifice to bond your clients to you? More than you suspect, because when a client considers the balance sheet in your relationship, the client almost always feels she has sacrificed more. Why is this?

Because the client makes sacrifices that you do not match.

She sacrifices control over the events—the delivery of food, advice, or assistance, for example—to you.

She also puts herself at the risk of the consequences—financial, professional, and personal—if the job is performed poorly. She cannot return a bad haircut, for example, or discover and recoup a tax overpayment.

And finally, she has sacrificed money. She has paid or burdened herself with an obligation to pay, while you may have sacrificed only time, of which you had excess capacity.

The sacrifice balance sheet weighs against you. Only your sacrifices will rebalance it, and only *major* sacrifices will create the feelings of obligation and reciprocity that can cement the relationship.

Most of us have heard the legendary service stories. The true tale of the Nordstrom salesperson who drove miles to the client's house to deliver the blue striped dress shirt he hoped to wear the next morning.

Or the Clear Lake Press salesperson who drove almost three hours to deliver an ink sample to a client.

Or the wonderful story of the San Francisco town car driver Effie, who picked up his client at the Garden Court Hotel in Palo Alto, heard his client gasp when he learned the plane left in twenty-nine minutes, raced to the airport, stopped the car at the terminal entrance, raced down the concourse to gate 42, and asked the Northwest Airline attendants to wait, his rider was just minutes behind.

These legends earn these companies their reputations as extraordinary services. All the stories have one element in common: the trait of the extraordinary service. Each involved a sacrifice.

To win devoted clients, sacrifice.

6. COMPLETENESS

Miracles happen—in this case, in Dallas, Texas.

You are leaving tomorrow for Dallas. You feel swamped and need pampering. You want four sets of dumbbells in your hotel room, to blow off some steam in private. You need a refill for your French-made pen that uses refills few American stationery stores carry. You feel a craving for organic orange juice, Tynant sparkling water (bottled in Wales), and the thirty-two-year-old Simon & Garfunkel album *Bookends*. Unfortunately, you realize you may not be able to order or enjoy any of them because you have to dash off a memo to salespeople in Israel and South Korea.

Let's face it: 99 percent of business travelers would laugh at the very idea of calling their hotel to request any of these items, much less all of them. You, however, decide that nothing is gained without venturing, so you give it a try. You call your hotel, the Mansion on Turtle Creek, with this wish list.

You arrive the next day. You open your hotel room door. The first thing you notice are the dumbbells, four of them, all silver, gleaming like mirrors below a windowsill. You walk to the desk and find the four pen refills sealed in a plastic pouch, and a new *Bookends* CD, thoughtfully removed from that too-tight shrink-wrap. You open your small refrigerator: Tynant water and organic orange juice. Then you notice that the paper on the desk that you assumed was just hotel stationery is not stationery at all. It is a copy of your memo—in English, Hebrew, and Korean.

The managers of the Mansion on Turtle Creek realize that one of the traits of extraordinary service is completeness. An extraordinary service can do whatever their client needs done. If they can't do it themselves, they can find someone who can.

The extraordinary service acts not just as a service. It acts as a resource.

As a simple contrast, distinguish this experience in Dallas from one in Fredericksburg, Virginia. The traveler checks in to a chain hotel on "franchise strip"—that section that looks exactly like those in 250 other American towns. The traveler knows better than to ask for Welsh water, but assumes he can ask directions to Highway 672. So he does. The woman behind the counter says, "Never heard of it."

The traveler naturally turns away briefly, knowing the woman will need several seconds to find her map and locate Highway 672.

He looks back and immediately realizes that the receptionist is done helping him. Not only doesn't she know where 672 is, she doesn't want to find out. Clearly, her minimal response to the man paying $78 per night should be, "Ask John Doe; he should be able to help you."

A day later, a Northwest Airlines flight attendant actually managed a ruder response. The traveler headed to the rest room, stopped at its door, noticed the attendant in the galley, and asked her, "Are you serving dinner on this flight?" The attendant pointed both hands, palms facing up, to the silver cart filled with dinners, and flashed the traveler her most vivid "What do you think *this* is, *stupid?*" expression.

These services represent the sublime to the ridiculous—though business travelers experience the ridiculous each day and the sublime rarely. At Turtle Creek, the employees will do everything you need. Without articulating it, you know that the hotel meets one of the eight tests of exceptional service: The Mansion is *complete*. Its employees "know how, or know who." You feel comfortable; you know you are in very good hands that have lifted a burden from you.

COMPLETENESS AND THE HARDWARE STORE

Are you complete? Can you help your client with any request reasonably related to your business?

Know how, or know who.

Let's imagine that you are in or near Needham, Massachusetts, and find yourself in the middle of the classic Bob Newhart "bomb" routine. In it, the poor local policeman—you, for our purpose— has come across a bomb on the beach. He calls headquarters. The officer there looks up bombs in the handbook and says:

"All you need is a Phillips 507 screwdriver with a plastic handle and a demagnetized head."

Now, you face long odds of finding that screwdriver anywhere, superstores included. But fortunately, you are just a short drive from Harvey's.

Harvey's has, or can get you, anything you want. In fact, with over $110 of inventory per square foot of the store, Harvey's probably has your screwdriver, no matter how screwy it sounds.

Harvey Katz defied all reason when he took over the store, buying even obscure hardware in huge quantities. This left him with huge inventory expenses and should have created nightmarish cash flow issues for a non-chain store.

But what has happened? A legend. People swarm from everywhere to shop at Harvey's. Once in the store, customers rarely buy only what they came for; the average Harvey's shopper spends almost 50 percent more per visit than the typical hardware shopper. So yes, Harvey's inventory comes pouring in, but it also goes pouring out.

Harvey's works. It generates almost three times the gross revenues of the average hardware store, with over 15 percent higher margins.

Harvey's works because it is *complete*. It has chosen a specific specialty and provides everything a customer for that service would want. The Harvey's customer enters the store knowing that Harvey's has the answer. Harvey's knows how or knows who, and the customer realizes that. The customer feels comfortable because Harvey's is complete.

You find Harvey'ses everywhere, flourishing. The East Bank Club in Chicago, for example, goes beyond the standard athletic club by including a clothes store, beauty salon, and car wash. Mystery bookstores from Portsmouth to Portland withstand the assaults of the giant chain bookstores by serving their market's obsession with the genre, offering huge, intelligent selections and equally obsessed service people who read mysteries fanatically too.

Be complete.

7. MAGIC WORDS

Thanks

"Attention must be paid," Willy Loman's wife demands on his behalf in *Death of a Salesman*, and the audience understands.

Each person feels Willy's pain: the hurt of being overlooked, ignored, uncounted. Some people strive for wealth, some for power, some for fame, but however different people's goals may be, we all share one wish: the desire to be regarded.

We know how much we value the respect and regard of others, yet in business, we constantly fail to extend it. For months and even years on end, our clients accept us, pay us, even refer us eagerly to others. What do we do in return? Oddly enough, what we should do is perfectly captured by that familiar phrase, "A simple thanks would be enough."

We forget. We fail. We move on to the next fire,

the next quota, the next goal; and we leave the client behind.

Yet when we're wearing our client's hat, do we ever feel thanked enough? Count the number of businesses that serve you each year. What thanks have they given you, other than the meaningless generic thank-you of the annual holiday card, mass mailed to everyone? The impact of that gesture on you was—what?

People crave one thing above all: appreciation.

To flourish in business, we must express one thing above all: our thanks.

Say thank you—often.

How Are You Doing?

Bell South Communications has hundreds of thousands of satisfied customers, and a knack for creating even more.

The people at Bell South have learned that if they perform a service competently, the majority of their customers will report that they are satisfied. But the company also learned they could increase that percentage dramatically—almost 40 percent, it turned out—by adding just one tiny step.

Within three days after they provide a service, a Bell South representative calls the customer and asks one question:

"How are you doing?"

The customers who received that follow-up call expressed significantly more satisfaction about the service when they were surveyed about it than those who got that call a week later.

One call—and one dramatic impact.

Bell South discovered a step that requires so little effort, you might well ask, "Why doesn't every service company call back within days?"

Well?

Just ask: "How are you doing?"

Welcome

You enter the Disney Beach Club Hotel. A gentleman named Art greets you. If you are especially lucky and are pushing a stroller, Art will stoop down, peek under the hood of it, fix his vivid brown eyes on your child, and say something magical:

"Oh, God's precious little gift."

You will love your stay. Research from the opposite end of America seems to prove it.

The executives at VetSmart, in Portland, Oregon, the veterinary facilities offered at most Petsmart stores, have carefully studied customer satisfaction. After surveying over 200,000 customers, they discovered what appeared to be the single key to client contentment:

The greeting.

Of the pet owners who reported that they felt "very welcome" when they entered VetSmart, 98 percent reported that they were very satisfied with their overall experience. No other factor—the reasonableness of the fee, the cleanliness of the facility, or the clarity with which the vet communicated to the pet owner—mattered remotely as much as the greeting.

The welcome to a service influences a person's perception of the *entire* experience. First impressions last—and great welcomes make a particularly lasting impression.

Among other influences, a sincere warm welcome suggests that the service cares about the person being welcomed. If something later goes wrong with the service, the person is likely to conclude, "This wasn't because they didn't care, or because I don't matter. It was an honest mistake."

Caring covers a multitude of sins—and a sincere welcome strongly demonstrates that caring. And more than any other single act, it comes close to ensuring your client's satisfaction.

How is your welcome?

How could it be made extraordinary?

Carnegie and Marinelli and Another Magic Word

Much to Dad's delight, I really did learn something in the summer of 1967.

That was the summer my near-desperate father, anguishing over my by-the-skin-of-my-teeth graduation from high school, decided to send me to Europe for the entire summer. Perhaps the Louvre and the Tower of London would awaken the sleeping scholar within, he thought.

For an eighteen-year-old who had never ventured east of Lewiston, Idaho, south of Coos Bay, Oregon, north of Vancouver, B.C., or west of our house peeking out over the Pacific Ocean, and who had never flown in a plane, Dad's proposal represented radical therapy.

Looking back, I remember many places and a few remarkable events from that trip, and four people by name. Three of them I remember because they traveled with my friend Des and me for the final five weeks. This is all I remember of them.

One was named Jim. He had studied engineering, lived in Winnipeg, and spoke French. That is all I remember about him.

I remember Joan. She taught Spanish in the New York public schools, and also spoke French. We danced until late one night in Spain.

I remember Corinna, from Sweden. She was a friend of Joan's. That's all I remember of her.

I spent five weeks with these three very nice and intelligent people, and remember almost nothing of them.

But this is what I remember of the fourth person, someone I spent only a few hours of six days in Denmark with.

Jim Marinelli was a second-year student at the University of Connecticut school of law. He was 6'1", 180 pounds, and was the perfect companion for a night in Copenhagen, one of the world's greatest towns for single people. Because in 1967, Jim Marinelli was one of the ten handsomest men in the Northern Hemisphere. You went with Jim to one of the city's nightclubs and within minutes, a dozen women would be hovering around, drawn there like ants to a gumdrop.

I remember his entire name and see him vividly not because of his ability to attract women, but because he possessed another gift. Jim Marinelli made you feel important. Despite the constant attention he received and the many ways he could have kept himself entertained night and day, Jim made near strangers feel like friends.

How?

I wasn't sure at first, but I knew it was something about how he addressed me. Some time later in the trip, I finally realized what it was. Jim used the magic word.

Jim said "Harry."

At every opportunity, Jim would use my name. "Harry, do you want to go to the Tivoli this afternoon?" "Let's go to the International Club tonight, Harry, what do you say?" (Dumb question, Jim. No, I will try to create my own magical magnetic force field alone, thanks.)

Simple, subtle: my name. And yet it worked. I remembered him, remembered his entire name, and felt bonded to him, special to him—because he called me by name.

Two years later, I visited my college library (just as Dad had hoped, the trip did arouse my curiosity about life). Browsing the first-floor stacks, I noticed a famous title: *How to Win Friends and Influence People* by Dale Carnegie. I picked it up, scanned it, and there it was: Jim Marinelli's secret. "[A] person's name is to that person the sweetest and the most important sound in any language."

Katharine Graham, the former publisher of the *Washington Post*, reveals just how much value people attach to their names. In her autobiography *Personal History*, Graham reveals a pet peeve: people who misspell her name. The person who can't be bothered to get her name right earns her enmity. We can presume that the person who always gets it right, and uses her name often, takes a giant step toward earning her friendship.

With apologies to Jim of Winnipeg, Joan of New York, and Corinna of Sweden, no one won a friend and so influenced a person like Jim Marinelli won and influenced me that summer more than thirty years ago.

Like a wonderful service provider, Jim made me feel important, largely because of one little word: mine.

__What's in a name? A better, stronger relationship.__

8. PASSION

Veer off Highway 95 into the forests north of Fredericksburg, Virginia, and you might come upon a secured gate. That gate separates you from a fascinating company—and lesson.

Inside, Personal Defensive Measures'* instructors are teaching Allied Signal and Amoco employees how to travel safely in Bogota. (No easy task. Seven people are kidnapped in Colombia every day.) Next door and up the hill, Kelly McCann and

---

*Recently, the name has been changed to Crucible for reasons this book's discussions of names have made clear.

several other instructors are teaching fifteen military officers the art of "Combatives"—a military euphemism for fighting. Very violent fighting.

(PDM's instructors, incidentally, know fighting. When they aren't on the lecture circuit and teaching people about personal safety, they lead missions into Kosovo and Bosnia, or raids on Colombia cocaine factories.)

Because you are fairly typical, you assume that McCann and company teach martial arts. For a perfectly good reason, however, they do not. As McCann observes, "Technique barely matters."

What does matter?

"Your head. Most people cannot fight because they do not want to, or cannot commit to winning. Fighting is ninety percent attitude. The good fighters have the mentality."

McCann has exposed the weakness of technique in anything—including marketing. You can follow some techniques and processes in marketing. For example, you can chart two desirable service attributes, one on the x axis and one on the y, and plot where you fall in the market. Or you can assess whether the choice of your service is rational or relatively emotional, and carefully considered or relatively impulsive. From those dots, you might try to make some key marketing decisions.

It will not matter. No one can trace any marketing breakthroughs to these techniques. At the same time, no one can ignore the extraordinary success of three organizations: the Marines, Nike, and Microsoft. What techniques have made them prosper?

None. Whatever techniques these organizations use are widely used by organizations that are failing. The most obvious difference—observable within seconds of your arrival inside the headquarters of any of these three—is their passion.

You can feel it in the halls.

(A revealing story. A visiting speaker at Microsoft told his audience that people everywhere succumb to the Lake Wobegon Effect—the tendency of people to assume they are doing better than they are at everything. Afterward, a member of the audience said he agreed that the Lake Wobegon Effect is pervasive outside Microsoft, but utterly absent inside it. "At Microsoft," he said, "the constant feeling is that whatever you are doing could always be made better.")

Spend a few moments in these companies' offices and you cannot resist the conclusion that the passion is airborne. These organizations radiate heat; they possess "an extraordinary commitment to better."

Many companies—learning organizations, some call them—know a lot; they nurture their intellectual capital. But thousands of fighters know how to fight—and can't.

Knowledge gets you into the game. Passion wins it.

Looking to hire a service almost ten years ago, we spoke with several candidates. One stood out. Like most prospects, we could not tell how excellent she was; we did not understand her specialty well enough to discern. What was palpable on meeting with her, however, was her passion. She radiated it. She had that quality that Ian Anderson, the former CEO of Unilever, ascribed to the great companies. She was *incandescent*.

Satisfied with her other qualifications, we retained her, and discovered something both peculiar and gratifying about passion. Passion spreads. Her passion for her work became our passion for her.

In the years that followed, we frequently encountered people who had used her company's services, and realized just how contagious her passion was. These clients, like us, adored her. They were not merely satisfied; they were utterly devoted. Her passion for her work created her client's passion for her.

Walk into the offices of one of these Ian Anderson firms, those that seem to radiate light and heat from the moment you enter. What is the source? Why does it appeal to you so strongly?

It is passion. The passion to do something extraordinary, as much as and often more than the actual achievement itself, drives employees and bonds their clients to them in ways other firms can only aspire to.

Excellence is not easily seen; it often escapes detection. The passion for it, however, is unmistakable. Prospects and clients know it when they see it.

Clients enjoy merely being in the presence of genuine passion. American corporations spend billions of dollars a year inviting people to speak to their company, simply to share their passion.

Passion is worth billions. It attracts clients. Even more clearly, it helps keep those clients—for life.

Acknowledgments

I am deep in debt; I owe millions to hundreds.

My debts are to Cliff Greene and Sue Crolick, who launched this book seven years ago, even more for who they are than for what they advised.

To Stephanie Prem, a perfect client, whose lessons from wealth management have helped crystallize this thinking.

To John Tillotson, who introduced me to seven critical laboratories for these ideas: 3000 Sandhill Road and its world of venture capital, and the Bay Area's six best restaurants: Chez Panisse, Fleur de Lys, the French Laundry, John Ash, the Lark Creek Inn, and L'Auberge de Soleil.

To my great teachers: Ron Rebholz, David Kennedy, James Robinson, William Clebsch, Gordon Wright, Robert Horn, John McPhee, Kurt Vonnegut, Harriet Evenson, E.B. White, John Tillman, William Zinsser, David Potter, and Stanford—all of it.

To the women and men who opened up themselves and their fine organizations: Peter Glanville of Wells Fargo; Mark Hughes of Bell South; Roger McGuinn of the Byrds; Roxanna Frost of Microsoft; Tim McClung of Go.edu; Said Hilal and Eugene Chen of Applied Medical; Heidi Vollkommer of Merck; the gang of 17 at Hewlett-Packard; Gene Tonculetto of the American Arbitration Association; Stan Barkey of State Farm Insurance; Meryl Golden of Progressive; Bruce Odza and Frank Accetuilli of EDS; John Wotring of Primrose; Carlton Schowe and Dick Schassberger of IMI; Susan Tinsley of Ivey Mechanical; Rob Fenza of Liberty Property Trust; Beth Miller of MetaMor; Rick Salzer of Allegiance; Joe Deckman and Micheala Diercks of Apogee; Larry Stratton and Rich Williams of ServiceMaster; Pete Thomas of Institutional Venture Partners; Jim Staples of Invisible Fencing and Right Management; Jim Van Loozen, Art Schealy, and U.S. Postmaster General Bill Henderson of the United States Postal Service; and Brian Graham of ADP.

To the exceptional advisers who demonstrate that Cal can listen to Stanford and vice versa: Peter Rocca, Dave Morehouse, and John Tillotson.

To Eric Madsen, Deb Miner, Sandra Simmons, Amy Quinlivan, Jennifer Reed, and Teresa Marrone, for making all of us better than each of us.

Acknowledgments

To the clients of a lifetime, literally and figuratively: Leftheris and Jane Papageourgiou of Hellenic Adventures, Clifford Greene of Greene Espel, and John Shultz of Ethical Investments and the Social Investment Forum.

To the pros at Warner Books for five special years: Rick Wolff, Mel Parker, Sharon Krassney, Dan Ambrosio, Jean Griffin, Andrew Fleischman, and Jimmy Franco. Thank you—all of you.

To Lynette Lamb and Ann Montague, for their wisdom, skill, and patience in spotting the order in all this chaos.

To Valerie and Dean, just because.

To Janice Eaves, whose gifts to my children I see every day, in their smiles.

To Becky Powell and David Macy Beckwith, who cared, come what may.

To Dr. Harry Beckwith, Jr., the Honorable James M. Burns, and the great athlete and gentleman, Clive Davies, my models.

To Sandra, at last, for gifts beyond listing.

231

To four more miracles: Harry IV, the natural; Will, the perfect world travel companion; Cole, the force of nature; and Cooper, the girl of my dreams.

And finally, to Mom. I feel that happiness and success grow from belief, a lesson she taught. Mom believed, even when all hope seemed gone, and her utter conviction became the whisper in my ear that kept me going. Her sacrifices for my education are reason enough to acknowledge her here. But those lessons from Stanford, remarkable though they were, mattered less than the single word Mom whispered that still echoes in my ears: *Believe*.